# Guide to Vocational Education and Training

Terry Hyland and
Christopher Winch

continuum

Continuum International Publishing Group
The Tower Building     80 Maiden Lane, Suite 704
11 York Road     New York, NY 10038
SE1 7NX

www.continuumbooks.com

*British Library Cataloguing-in-Publication Data*
A catalogue record for this book is available from the British Library.

ISBN: 0826490476 (paperback)

*Library of Congress Cataloging-in-Publication Data*
A catalog record for this book is available from the Library of Congress.

Typeset by YHT Ltd, London
Printed and bound in Great Britain by Ashford Colour Press Ltd, Gosport, Hants.

# Contents

For Josephine – the most skillful, mindful and committed vocational practitioner I have ever met.

Terry

.

# Series Foreword

## THE ESSENTIAL FE TOOLKIT SERIES

## Jill Jameson
## Series Editor

*In the autumn of 1974, a young woman newly arrived from Africa landed in Devon to embark on a new life in England. Having travelled half way round the world, she still longed for sunny Zimbabwe. Not sure what career to follow, she took a part-time job teaching EFL to Finnish students. Enjoying this, she studied thereafter for a PGCE at the University of Nottingham in Ted Wragg's Education Dept. After teaching in secondary schools, she returned to university in Cambridge, and, having graduated, took a job in ILEA in 1984 in adult education. She loved it: there was something about adult ed. that woke her up, made her feel fully alive, newly aware of all the lifelong learning journeys being followed by so many students and staff around her. The adult community centre she worked in was a joyful place for diverse multi-ethnic communities. Everyone was cared for, including 90-year-olds in wheelchairs, toddlers in the crèche, ESOL refugees, city accountants in business suits and university-level graphic design students. In her eyes, the centre was an educational ideal, a remarkable place in which, gradually, everyone was helped to learn to be who they wanted to be. This was the Chequer Centre, Finsbury, EC1, the 'red house', as her daughter saw it, toddling in from the crèche. And so began the story of a long interest in further education that was to last for many years. ... Why, if they did such good work for so many, were FE centres so under-funded and unrecognized, so under-appreciated?*

It is with delight that, 32 years after the above story began, I write the Foreword to The Essential FE Toolkit, Continuum's new book series of 24 books on further education (FE) for teachers and college leaders. The idea behind the Toolkit is to provide a comprehensive guide to FE in a series of compact, readable books. The suite of 24 individual books are gathered together to provide the practitioner with an overall FE toolkit in specialist, fact-filled volumes designed to be easily accessible, written by experts with significant knowledge and experience in their individual fields. All of the authors have in-depth understanding of further education. But – '*Why is further education important? Why does it merit a whole series to be written about it?*' you may ask.

At the Association of Colleges Annual Conference in 2005, in a humorous speech to college principals, John Brennan said that, whereas in 1995 further education was a 'political back-water', by 2005 FE had become 'mainstream'. John recalled that, since 1995, there had been '36 separate Government or Government-sponsored reports or white papers specifically devoted to the post-16 sector'. In our recent regional research report (2006) for the Learning and Skills Development Agency, my co-author Yvonne Hillier and I noted that it was no longer 'raining policy' in FE, as we had described earlier (Hillier and Jameson, 2003): there is now a torrent of new initiatives. We thought, in 2003, that an umbrella would suffice to protect you. We'd now recommend buying a boat to navigate these choppy waters, as it looks as if John Brennan's 'mainstream' FE, combined with a tidal wave of government policies, will soon lead to a flood of new interest in the sector, rather than end any time soon.

There are good reasons for all this government attention on further education. In 2004/05, student numbers in Learning and Skills Council (LSC)-funded further education increased to 4.2 million, total college income was around £6.1 billion, and the average college had an annual turnover of £15 million. Further education has rapidly increased in national significance regarding the need for ever greater achievements in UK education and skills training for millions of learners, providing qualifications and workforce training to feed a UK national economy hungrily in competition with other Organisation for Economic Co-operation and Development (OECD) nations. The 120 recommendations of the Foster Review (2005) therefore in the main encourage colleges to focus their work on vocational skills, social inclusion and achieving academic progress. This series is here to consider all three of these areas and more.

The series is written for teaching practitioners, leaders and managers in the 572 FE/LSC-funded institutions in the UK, including FE colleges, adult education and sixth-form institutions, prison education departments, training and workforce development units, local education authorities and community agencies. The series is also written for PGCE/Cert Ed/City & Guilds Initial and continuing professional development (CPD) teacher trainees in universities in the UK, USA, Canada, Australia, New Zealand and beyond. It will also be of interest to staff in the 600 Jobcentre Plus providers in the UK and to many private training organizations. All may find this series of use and interest in learning about FE educational practice in the 24 different areas of these specialist books from experts in the field.

Our use of this somewhat fuzzy term 'practitioners' includes staff in the FE/LSC-funded sector who engage in professional practice in governance, leadership, management, teaching, training, financial and administration services, student support services, ICT and MIS technical support, librarianship, learning resources, marketing, research and development, nursery and crèche services, community and business support, transport and estates management. It is also intended to include staff in a host of other FE services including work-related training, catering, outreach and specialist health, diagnostic additional learning support, pastoral and religious support for students. Updating staff in professional practice is critically important at a time of such continuing radical policy-driven change, and we are pleased to contribute to this nationally and internationally.

We are also privileged to have an exceptional range of authors writing for the series. Many of our series authors are renowned for their work in further education, having worked in the sector for thirty years or more. Some have received OBE or CBE honours, professorships, fellowships and awards for contributions they have made to further education. All have demonstrated a commitment to FE that makes their books come alive with a kind of wise guidance for the reader. Sometimes this is tinged with world-weariness, sometimes with sympathy, humour or excitement. Sometimes the books are just plain clever or a fascinating read, to guide practitioners of the future who will read these works. Together, the books make up a considerable portfolio of assets for you to take with you through your journeys in further education. We hope the experience of reading the books will be interesting, instructive and pleasurable and that experience gained from them will last, renewed, for many seasons.

It has been wonderful to work with all of the authors and with Continuum's UK Education Publisher, Alexandra Webster, on this series. The exhilarating opportunity of developing such a comprehensive toolkit of books probably comes once in a lifetime, if at all. I am privileged to have had this rare opportunity, and I thank the publishers, authors and other contributors to the series for making these books come to life with their fantastic contributions to FE.

Dr Jill Jameson
Series Editor
March 2006

# Series Introduction

## THE ESSENTIAL FE TOOLKIT SERIES

## Jill Jameson
## Series Editor

### *A Guide to Vocational Education and Training* – Terry Hyland and Christopher Winch

*Groundhog Day* describes the endlessly repeating cycle of relived history experienced by TV weatherman Phil Connors, played by Bill Murray in the 1993 film. Phil is caught in a time-loop in which he experiences the same day again and again – Groundhog Day (February 2). Phil's increasing awareness of *déjà vu* allows him space to recognize and address key defects in his character. Listening to the advice of Rita, his producer, he breaks out from an egotistical, cynical approach to life and learns how to be a more compassionate and generous person, encompassing along the way developments in musical expertise, ice sculpture and the ability genuinely to love others. These self-improvements enable him to find love with Rita, and he wakes up, a better person, to discover at last that time has moved on: it is now February 3rd.

The metaphor of the *Groundhog Day* time-loop is one of the themes underpinning this fascinating new book from the Essential FE Toolkit Series, *A Guide to Vocational Education and Training* by Professor Christopher Winch and Professor Terry Hyland. This expert, readable guide to vocational education and training (VET) in England traces the endlessly repeating problems which have, again and again, stunted progression and growth in VET in England over past decades. How can we break out of the loop of cyclical frustrated attempts to redress the vocational/academic divide in which VET in FE in England seems to be trapped?

Christopher and Terry provide us with an excellent analysis of the overall situation affecting vocational education and training, supplemented by positive suggestions for a more promising future for VET. The authors describe the history and current state of VET by locating the origins of the vocational/academic divide in philosophical distinctions about the relative value of pure and applied knowledge which date back to Ancient Greece. They demonstrate how these ideas informed and influenced English education: a mass national system was established in which prejudices downplaying the role of VET were enshrined.

The authors report that, although there is little philosophical justification for a vocational/academic divide, links between knowledge differentiation and social stratification have consistently beleaguered attempts to reconcile divisions and achieve parity of esteem for vocational studies. VET policy reform is now ever higher on the government agenda, in view of its role in economic competitiveness: the book analyses the complex, problematic 'skills agenda' including new developments in the English system of VET, comparing this somewhat unfavourably with European counterparts, notably in Germany and France.

The book's examination of the recent past and current state of vocational policy, theory and practice in England reflects on the implications of recent policy developments, including the government White Papers on FE (2005, 2006), Foster Review (2005c), Skills Review (2005) and the 14–19 qualifications curriculum reform (2005). The authors observe that the 'history of VET in England in the twentieth century can be viewed as a series of short-lived and unsatisfactory attempts to reform the system in the light of a number of persistent problems (continuing into the present century with skills strategies and FE policy papers; DfES, 2006a, 2006b) which, at the time of writing, seem to be worsening (Hayward, 1995; Keep, 2006).'

From this somewhat depressingly trapped-in situation, the authors offer us a refreshing new way out of the VET time-loop in their insightful conclusion, which provides specific recommendations to achieve a complete turnaround in vocational education and training.

This excellent book on VET in England, written by two professors from the University of Bolton and King's College, University of London, both of whom have exceptional knowledge of this field, is a 'must-read' for FE leaders, managers, policy-makers, employers, trainers and all other personnel charged with promoting the 'skills agenda' in further education.

I highly recommend it to you.

Dr Jill Jameson
Director of Research
School of Education and Training
University of Greenwich
j.jameson@gre.ac.uk

# 1 Vocational Education and Training in England: 'Will Cinderella Ever Make It to the Ball?'

## Background: the vocational/academic divide

Echoing many similar observations over the years about English vocational education and training (VET), Maclure (1991) noted the 'historic failure of English education to integrate the academic and the practical, the general and the vocational' (p. 28). Current policy-makers are still struggling with this so-called vocational/academic divide – most recently in the Tomlinson report on the reform of the 14–19 curriculum and qualifications structure (DfES, 2004a) and the government White Paper responding to this (DfES, 2005a) – though the problems in this sphere are by no means of recent origin.

Attempts to enhance the status of VET and create parity of value and esteem for vocational as against academic learning and qualifications go back at least as far as the last quarter of the nineteenth century when the Royal Commission on Technical Instruction was established to make recommendations for the improvement of the English system in the light of the perceived superiority of European systems (Musgrave, 1970). Since then, the State's response to problems in this field has typically been one of 'crisis management ... giving rise to schemes and initiatives designed to limit the social damage which followed de-industrialisation' (Esland, 1990, p. v). More recently, in the introduction to the blueprint document which was to establish the then University for Industry (now known as *Learndirect* without any university claims), Hillman (1997) noted that:

> Deficiencies in British education and training have been a cause for concern for policy-makers for 150 years ... there has been a flurry of reforms in the last ten years ... an array of short-term and narrowly-focused initiatives. (p. 29)

Among this 'flurry of reforms' were the many schemes asso-
ciated with the 'new vocationalism' (Hyland, 1999) of the
1980s and 1990s: the Technical and Vocational Education
Initiative for schools, Youth Training Schemes, General and
National Vocational Qualifications (G/NVQs), Training
Credits and Training and Enterprise Councils. Only time will
tell whether the latest batch of reforms under the Labour
government's lifelong learning agenda (originally set out in *The
Learning Age*, DfEE, 1998) – *Learndirect*, New Deal Welfare to
Work programmes, Curriculum 2000, Vocational GCSEs/
A-levels, Learning and Skills Councils (LSCs), reconstructed
Modern Apprenticeships and 14–19 reorganization – will have
any more success than previous measures. Certainly, there is
little indication that the perennial problems of VET – the
subordinate status of vocational studies, low employer investment in VET, a relatively low-skilled workforce and the lack of
a national, coherent education and training system (Ainley,
1999; Hyland, 1999) – are being effectively tackled by the
recent legislation.

## Mapping the divide

The British (nowadays, specifically English) malaise is not just
the gulf between vocational and academic education but the
extremely inferior, second-class status attached to vocational/
practical learning as against academic/liberal pursuits (other
aspects of the so-called 'malaise' will be mentioned in later
chapters comparing the English system with its Continental
counterparts). When the then Secretary of State for Education
complained in 2000 about the fact that teachers have for too
long 'had to contend with an elitist academic culture which has
failed to value technical study' (DfEE, 2000a, para. 36) he was
alluding to prejudices which have existed for centuries and
which still influence policy-makers and educators at all levels.

This was recently vividly demonstrated in Raggatt and
Williams's (1999) examination of the development and reform
of vocational qualifications in the 1980s and 1990s, which
involved a detailed analysis of legislation combined with
interviews with leading players in the field. They noted that

officials in the former Department of Education and Science (DES, now the DfES – Department for Education and Skills) freely admitted that the 'whole area of vocational education, training and qualifications was ... a backwater in the DES', and an education minister commented that:

> People in the DES had never come across it [vocational education]. They did not expect their children to come across it ... So there was a complete cultural problem with the status of vocational education. (*ibid.*, p. 183)

The fact that, as other commentators have observed in the past, discussions of VET are always somehow about 'other people's children' serves to illustrate graphically what Lewis (1991) has called the 'historical problem of vocational education' which is its subordinate status in relation to academic studies and the fact that it 'has traditionally been viewed in class terms' (pp. 96–7).

Examining the historical development of vocational studies in English schools, Coffey (1992) noted that its 'place and scope ... has been sparse, limited in intent and fragmented'. Lewis (1991) suggests that 'whether in the developed or developing world ... vocational education has been conceived of as being unworthy of the elite, and more suited to the oppressed or unprivileged class' (p. 97). In a similar vein, Skilbeck *et al.* (1994) comment that, in England and Wales, the 'educational tradition has been inhospitable to a broad and comprehensive vocational philosophy', in spite of the fact that there has recently been a 'resurgence of interest in the world's industrialised countries in the vocational dimension of education' (pp. 22, 138).

## Origins of the divide

If educational processes are viewed as a general form of 'upbringing' (White, 1997, pp. 82–3), then vocational learning is as old and – given its importance to human survival and reproduction – arguably older than any other form of education. As Coffey (1992) observes, all early education can be said to have had an 'explicit vocational function' in that:

Economic life was primarily sustained by the passing on of manual skills from one generation to the next. Most people were educated 'on the job', in particular by experiencing some form of formal or informal apprenticeship. (p. 11)

Both the formal and the informal educational practices of early societies – with the vocational function of inculcating the knowledge, skills and values needed for survival – must have included the passing on to young people of the main elements of hunting, fishing, farming, making clothing and caring for children. Benjamin's famous 'Saber-Tooth curriculum' (1939), which consisted of the skills of fish-grabbing, horse-clubbing and saber-tooth tiger-scaring – though clearly fictitious and allegorical in purpose – is probably a reasonably accurate account of how such early VET practices eventually came to be formalized and systematized as tribes and communities developed religious, puberty and organizational/leadership mores and rituals.

Since such vocational practices seem to be not just natural but also absolutely vital for human survival and progress, the intriguing question is why educational processes came to be hierarchically stratified and differentiated, with distinctions of status and prestige which generally disfavour vocational pursuits. After all, there is a broad consensus that vocational education originally had pride of place in the development of formal systems. Williams (1961), for instance, argues that the 'first English schools, from the late 6th century, had a primarily vocational intention' (p. 167) and, according to Lawson and Silver (1978), even the liberal studies of the early grammar schools can be said to have had a markedly vocational thrust since its principal purpose was to equip people 'for careers as teachers, preachers, civil and canon lawyers, officials and administrators' (p. 31). Indeed, the 'staple' of the liberal studies curriculum, Latin language study, is described as a 'vocational skill' (ibid., p. 48) and its function as a Renaissance puberty rite – insofar as it 'strengthened and toughened the mind' (Ong, 1970, p. 247) – has been well documented, as has the parallel 'apprenticeship' status of the Bachelor degree in medieval universities in the preparation for Master status (Carr, 1997).

Thus, the conception of work-based learning for induction into a vocational field can be seen to apply to both liberal and vocational traditions.

Given all this, the idea that the vocational aspect of education would eventually come to have a second-rate status, subordinate to general, academic studies, seems extraordinarily surprising. How can this be explained? The evolution of Benjamin's 'saber-tooth curriculum' gives us some clues. As New-Fist, one of the more thoughtful members of the Chellean community, started to reflect on the knowledge and skills necessary for the survival of his tribe − fish-grabbing with bare hands, woolly horse-clubbing and saber-tooth tiger-scaring − he saw the advantages of teaching these vital arts to his children and proposed a system of education and training consisting of these three main elements.

For a long time the conservative members of the tribe resisted these suggestions, but eventually − as New-Fist's practice clearly showed the benefits gained by teaching children rather than trusting to luck − the pioneer educator's ideas were adopted. Unfortunately, very soon after the saber-tooth curriculum had been formalized, a new ice age came over the land and the old skills were rendered obsolete. However, in spite of the fact that the tribe's survival now depended totally upon the new crafts of catching fish with nets, building snares to catch antelopes and killing bears, the old curriculum remained unchanged. The venerable tribal elders blocked all demands for curriculum reform by declaring that if the would-be reformers only knew the difference between education and training, they 'would know that the essence of true education is timelessness ... You must know that there are some eternal verities ... and the saber-tooth curriculum is one of them!' (Benjamin, 1975, pp. 13–14).

This account serves to demonstrate graphically − by means of analogic narrative more powerful than historical sources − the likely origins of the vocational/academic divide in a way which highlights the origins of the dualisms of education and training, the general and the practical, in addition to the linking of cultural studies with general virtue and practical pursuits with utilitarian values. In a similar vein, Pinker's (1998) evolutionary account of the development of the human mind explains how the 'more biologically frivolous and vain the activity, the more people exalt it' (p. 521). Many of the activities that humans consider intrinsically valuable can be viewed as 'non-adaptive by-products' of having minds such as ours. Consequently, the more ideas and pursuits are distanced from adaptive survival purposes, the more they tend to be valued in societies in which survival is no longer the primary concern. This can help us to understand why certain educational practices (thought of as liberal or academic) connected with leisure and culture came to be prized more highly than others (labelled vocational) concerned with work, reproduction and survival.

## Vocational/academic divisions

These hierarchical curriculum divisions, eventually linked to social status and stratification, were later codified precisely by Dewey (1916/1966) in his attempts to break down the 'antithesis of vocational and cultural education' based on the false oppositions of 'labour and leisure, theory and practice, body and mind' (p. 306).

Although there may be a tendency to regard the vocational/academic divide in England as a relatively recent phenomenon – perhaps arising out of the different schooling practices enshrined in the 1944 Education Act – the roots of this dichotomy can be traced much further back. As Silver and Brennan (1988) put it: 'education and training, theory and practice, the liberal and the vocational – the polarities have centuries of turbulent history' (p. 3).

Schofield (1972) locates the original source of liberal education in those activities associated with 'freeing the mind from error' (pp. 149–50) which has its roots in Plato's distinction between 'genuine' knowledge (acquired through rational reflection) and mere 'opinion' (acquired for specific, practical purposes). Moreover, such hierarchical divisions were from the outset connected directly with social class stratification which carried with it a whole range of relative, differential values about educational activities. For example, in Plato's *Republic*, the relative values accorded to the 'Forms' of knowledge are fully realized in the various kinds of education provided for rulers, guardians and workers in the ideal state. The 'foundation myth' of this state suggests that God 'added gold to the composition of those of you who are qualified to be rulers ... he put silver in the auxiliaries, and iron and bronze in farmers and the rest' (Lee, 1965, p. 160). Similarly, in *The Politics*, Aristotle offers an account of rival educational aims and purposes – essentially valuing disinterested theory above applied practical knowledge – which is uncannily similar to the vocational/ academic (technical/liberal) discourse that has characterized educational debates since the establishment of state schooling in England in the nineteenth century (Sinclair, 1962).

Once such hierarchical and normative distinctions had been made by philosophers, it was almost inevitable that they would come to be linked – through formal systems of education – with political power and social stratification. As Schofield (1972) explains:

> The passing of time merely emphasised the distinctions which Plato made. Studies which were valuable in themselves, especially the Classics, became associated with the privileged class or elite in society. They were directly related to the concept of a courtier, a gentleman, a man of affairs, and later the public schools. Liberal education always carried with it a suggestion of privilege and privileged position, of not needing to work for one's living. (pp. 151–2)

The linking of such ideals to classical studies and the public school/university elite in nineteenth-century England (which produced the politically influential who were to define the nature of mass compulsory schooling after 1870) served to establish a class-dominated, bifurcated system in which vocational studies were always subordinate to academic pursuits. Educational debate from this time was distorted by irrational prejudices which, as Skilbeck *et al.* (1994) argue, were 'compounded by anti-democratic and arcadian ideals' (p. 160) which have stood in the way of the development of a national, unified system of education in England in which vocational studies and the preparation for working life have their proper place.

## Reconciling divisions

Since the philosophical origins of the vocational/academic dichotomy can be traced back to fundamental distinctions between pure (disinterested) and applied (instrumental) knowledge and understanding, many strategies for reconciling the divisions have sought to show either that so-called liberal pursuits can be construed in vocational terms or, more commonly, that vocational studies can in fact be interpreted in terms of liberal/academic education. An interesting early example of this revisionism can be seen in Adams's (1933) *Modern Developments in Educational Practice* which insists that 'all education must affect our future life either adversely or favourably, and to that extent all education is vocational, as preparing us for the vocation of life' (p. 50). A more recent example of this approach is Silver and Brennan's (1988) advocacy of 'liberal vocationalism' in higher education involving the introduction of hybrid courses combining arts and science subjects, in addition to incorporating liberal/general educational elements in vocational fields such as engineering and business studies.

At another level, such strategies are not unlike the general/liberal studies introduced into further education (FE) colleges in the 1950s and 1960s – resurrected in diluted form as core and key skills in contemporary post-school education (Hyland, 1999) – and which show that 'pre-vocational' skills such as literacy and numeracy are a necessary prerequisite for access to *any* educational activity whether it is labelled vocational or academic. Similar sentiments inspire Winch's (1995) argument that 'education needs training' since all educational pursuits are dependent upon training in basic skills, and also Dearden's (1990) suggestion that there are no a priori reasons why education and training should not be compatible because:

> a process of training could be liberally conceived in such a way as to explore relevant aspects of understanding, and in a way which satisfies the internal standards of truth and accuracy. (p. 93)

A key aspect of all such perspectives consists in demonstrating that liberal and vocational activities have many features in common. Thus, we have R. S. Peters (1978) observing that both theoretical and practical pursuits may be engaged in 'for their own sakes' (p. 9) and Walsh (1978) arguing that 'once the real values of liberal pursuits are stated and classified ... we can find the same values in practical pursuits' (p. 62). In a similar vein, Williams (1994), while (quite rightly) not 'denying the distinction between liberal and vocational learning or the existence of genuine tensions between them', observes that:

> learning for its own sake and learning for vocational purposes need not be conceived of as mutually exclusive activities. The distinction between liberal and vocational learning does not imply that what is vocationally useful cannot be personally satisfying and enriching or that what is personally satisfying and enriching cannot be useful. (pp. 97–8)

Pring (1995) makes use of similar ideas in suggesting that a reconstructed conception of vocational studies can be a 'way into those forms of knowledge through which a person is freed from ignorance and opened to new imaginings, new possibilities' (p. 189).

As mentioned above, the first grammar schools and universities had a clear vocational function in preparing people for professions and – particularly in teaching, medicine and the law – there is no necessary incompatibility between the intrinsically valuable (so-called pure) knowledge and the extrinsically useful (so-called applied) knowledge. In support of such compatibilist ideas it is worth noting that – in terms of the links between knowledge and its application – it is, in practice, very difficult to draw hard and fast distinctions between pure and applied studies, between the intrinsic and the instrumental, the contemplative intellectual and the practical doer. Who could have predicted, for example, that Dirac's abstruse research resulting in the discovery of anti-matter would one day lead to a highly effective method for detecting tumours (Goddard, 1999) or that Rousseau's ideas about popular sovereignty would eventually inspire the makers of the French Revolution (Salvemini, 1965).

Moreover, it is surely worth noting that one common unifying element in relation to the main divisions in this sphere – vocational/academic, general, technical, theory/practice, mind/body – is precisely and centrally the process and activity of *learning*. What matters, therefore, is perhaps not so much any bridging of divides but the adoption of strategies which ensure that vocational learning is rich, deep and facilitates that progression and continuity essential to learning careers, working life and lifelong learning needs and objectives. It is this idea of a 'learning career' – illustrated fully in Bloomer's (1996) conception of 'studentship' through which 'students can exert influence over the curriculum in the creation and confirmation of their own personal careers' (p. 140) – which deserves a central place in strategies designed to enhance vocational studies. If such a conception of learning – whether formal or informal, work-based or college-based – is located within a framework informed by Dewey's broad conception of vocational education as a range of processes/activities designed to 'stress the full intellectual and social meaning of a vocation' (1966, p. 316), then this might herald the beginning of a journey which leads to the elusive parity of esteem for VET in the English education system.

## Summary and conclusion

The origins of the vocational/academic divide in England can be located in philosophical distinctions about the relative value of pure and applied knowledge dating back to Ancient Greece. As these ideas came to inform and influence English education, a mass national system was established in which such prejudices were enshrined. In spite of the fact that there is little philosophical justification for the vocational/academic divide, the links between knowledge differentiation and social stratification have severely hampered attempts to reconcile divisions and establish parity of esteem for vocational studies. Policy reform is still ongoing and later chapters – set against the analysis and description of the English system of VET compared with its counterparts in Continental Europe – will examine the recent past and current state of vocational policy, theory and practice in England.

# 2 'Groundhog Day': The History and Development of VET in England

## Historical background

Until late medieval times most English schools – including, at this time, the public schools such as Winchester and Rugby (Leach, 1904) – were essentially 'common' schools which accepted 'poor' scholars alongside the sons of the gentry and charged very small fees. In the theory of education developed by Erasmus in the sixteenth century – though this was still firmly rooted in the traditional classicist mould – there emerges the idea that a common schooling should be provided for all young people (though mainly boys rather than girls!) with the ultimate educational aim of 'world citizenship' (Curtis and Boultwood, 1970, pp. 129–30). However, all this was soon to change. As Kenneth Richmond (1945) explains:

> The conviction that there are two distinct brands of education, one for the rulers and another for commoners, dates from the sixteenth century. The divergence was not at first clearly marked; under the Stuarts, for example, the rich were far less cut off from intermingling with other classes in the schools than they are today; but the eighteenth century confirmed it as a hard-and-fast rule. Only towards the close of this period was there any observable distinction between the old Grammar Schools and Public Schools. (p. 53)

As mentioned in Chapter 1, the notion of a differential education system which incorporates separate and distinctive schooling for the rulers and the ruled is as old as Plato's *Republic*. Kenneth Richmond's observation represents the practical implementation of these practices in the English system. For the status of vocational studies, such stratification was disastrous since it emphasized not only the divisions between vocational and liberal studies but also the designation of vocational learning as second-rate and inferior to general education.

During the Renaissance and Reformation periods, although higher education was dominated by a self-perpetuating aristocratic elite, the grammar schools did still provide for the sons of wealthy tradesmen. By the eighteenth century, many of them had a 'quite varied social composition with some broadening of the curriculum, particularly in mathematics and natural science' (Williams, 1961, p. 154). However, although the:

> eighteenth century is remarkable for the growth of a number of new vocational academies serving commerce, engineering, the arts and the armed services ... of the new professions, particularly in science, engineering and the arts, a majority of entrants were trained outside the universities, as were also most of the new merchants and manufacturers. (*Ibid.*, p. 155)

In fact, the university curriculum in the main was to remain ossified in the classical tradition until the reform of Oxford and Cambridge in the nineteenth century and the growth of provincial institutions in the twentieth century (Barnard, 1961).

Until the nineteenth century – in spite of the massive upheaval and social/economic change generated from around 1750 by the Industrial Revolution (Plumb, 1961) – working-class education remained unplanned with a 'haphazard system of parish and private adventure schools' and, paralleling the growing urbanization of working people, the emergence of the Charity School movement concerned mainly with the 'moral rescue as opposed to the moral instruction of the poor' (Williams, 1961, p. 155). An Act of 1576 had empowered magistrates to establish workhouse schools 'to the intent that youth might be accustomed and brought up in labour and then not likely to grow to be idle rogues' (Coffey, 1992, p. 26). In the early eighteenth century, the Society for Promoting Christian Knowledge recommended a half-time education system – designed to prepare boys for apprenticeship and girls for domestic service – whereby children devoted alternate days to work and school (Simon, 1974).

The Industrial Revolution was neither caused nor accompanied by the growth of formal education (Dore, 1976). Countries such as France and Prussia had established compulsory state schooling long before England yet did not industrialize until well after the British Industrial Revolution. As Ashby (1958) explains:

> The Industrial Revolution was accomplished by hard heads and clever fingers. Men like Bramah and Maudslay, Arkwright and Crompton, the Darbys of Coalbrookdale and Neilson of Glasgow, had no systematic education in science or technology. Britain's industrial strength lay in its amateurs and self-made men ... formal education of any sort was a negligible factor in its success. The schools attended by the prosperous classes followed a curriculum which had scarcely changed since the school days of John Milton two centuries earlier. (p. 50)

In fact, as Coffey (1992) argues, in spite of the revolutionary changes, education in the early nineteenth century bore little connection with the world of work and 'the economy did not to any noticeable extent depend upon the educational system for a supply of skilled artisans' (p. 27).

At the Great Exhibition held at the Crystal Palace in 1851 Britain's status as the 'foremost industrial nation' (Musgrave, 1970, p. 144) was on display for all to view. However, by the time of the Paris Exhibition of 1867, Dr Lyon Playfair was moved to write to the Taunton Commission (then considering the state of technical education) urging them to consider the state of 'scientific instruction' as part of their remit so as to help Britain keep pace with foreign competition (*ibid.*). Following the report of the Royal Commission on Scientific Instruction in 1884, a Technical Instruction Act was passed by Parliament in 1889 which legislated for:

> instruction in the principles of science and art applicable to industries, and in the application of specific branches of science and art to specific industries or employments. It shall not include the teaching of any trade or industry or employment. (Musgrave, 1964, p. 106)

The markedly theoretical thrust of the Act reflected both the territorial power of the craft guilds concerned to protect occupational secrecy and also the state of the debate about the differences between technical education (principles) and technical instruction (practice). This ambiguity exacerbated the class divisions both *between* vocational and general education and *within* vocational/technical education. As Musgrave notes, 'technical education for the upper levels of the labour force might still be seen in terms of general principles, but at the lower levels to teach practice was now becoming the custom' (*Ibid.*, p. 109).

In terms of state schooling in general, Forster's Elementary Education Act of 1870 (effectively establishing compulsory state schooling in Britain for the first time) had 'primarily an economic purpose' (Coffey, 1992, p. 50). Introducing the bill in the House of Commons in February 1870, Forster argued that:

> Upon the speedy provision of elementary education depends our industrial prosperity. It is of no use trying to give technical teaching to our artisans without elementary education; uneducated labourers – and many of our labourers are uneducated – are, for the most part, unskilled labourers, and if we leave our workfolk any longer unskilled ... they will become overmatched in the competition of the world. (Maclure, 1973, pp. 99–100)

If we replace 'elementary education' with 'basic skills' and substitute 'global competitiveness' for the 'competition of the world', it is astonishing how Forster's justification of elementary schooling matches in all important particulars the arguments advanced by policy-makers and DfES officials over the last decade or so.

Educators inclined towards pessimism might well reflect on how little progress has been made in 135 years of state education in England!

The Balfour Education Act of 1902 effectively established an embryonic national system of education – based on the principle of 'central and local government partnership' (Kenneth Richmond, 1945, p. 88) – which characterized the British system until the 1988 Education Reform Act. In the early years of the twentieth century there was a shift of emphasis from elementary to secondary provision. However, when a recognizably national secondary system finally emerged in England in the 1920s and 1930s it was constrained by the hierarchical and stratified conceptions of the nineteenth-century curriculum in which vocational studies had a subordinate place.

Informed by a 'spiritually predestined class system' (Coffey, 1992, p. 62) the national system was at the outset dominated by class interests and divisions and could not escape the power relationships and educational values linked to such divisions (Green, 1990).

This nineteenth-century legacy was clearly described by Kenneth Richmond (1945):

> The Victorian attitude to education was much the same as it was to all other public services: it has its First-Class compartments, the Public Schools with the doors and windows locked against riff-raff; its Second-Class, the old Grammar schools intended for the sons of the bourgeoisie, the professions; its Third-Class, the Elementary Schools for the 'lower orders', the artisans. (p. 90)

Such divisiveness and rigid stratification − continuing through the tripartite organization of schooling following the 1944 Education Act and beyond − effectively prevented the emergence of any idea of a 'common school' for all young people, and ensured that the 'perennial liberal versus utilitarian debate continued to be fought mainly on class lines' (Coffey, 1992, p. 73). Moreover, the long-established British 'resistance to the provision of technical education at the secondary stage' (Lester Smith, 1966, p. 209) meant that not even the nineteenth-century conception of 'artisanship' could develop to ensure the secondary schooling might, as a basic minimum, come to incorporate some sort of meaningful or worthwhile form of vocational studies.

The technical schools established in the wake of the 1944 Education Act − like the provision for day-continuation classes for young people up to the age of 18 following the 1918 Education Act − were short-lived, partly because of the 'hostility of both parents and employers of labour' (Dent, 1968,

p. 36) and partly because of the continued dominance of academic/liberal notions of what counts as 'genuine' education at the secondary level. In summarizing developments in schooling between 1922 and 1947, Coffey (1992) concluded that although

> it emerged that it was regarded as an important part of the school's business to prepare pupils for the world of work ... a vocational bias in the curriculum and explicit skill training for occupations appeared ... only in less prestigious secondary schools ... Vocational and practical subjects in general had not attained the importance of the more prestigious 'academic' and 'pure' subjects. (p. 153)

This second-class status of vocational studies – accompanied by its neglect and lack of development during the massive expansion of secondary-level academic examinations in the post-1945 settlement – effectively prevented either the bridging of the vocational/academic divide or the upgrading of the vocational aspect of education. As McCulloch (1986) noted, the 'technical and vocational end of education somehow got lost' in the relentless 'drives towards comprehensives' (p. 129) in the 1960s, a loss described by Halsey *et al.* (1980) as 'one of the tragedies of British education after the second war' (p. 214).

## Tragic narratives

The history of vocational studies in the post–1945 period has been fully documented and analysed by a wide range of commentators (Sheldrake and Vickerstaff, 1987; Evans, 1992; Ainley, 1988, 1990, 1999; Hyland, 1999; Winch, 2000). Echoing the comment made above by Halsey *et al.*, these developments may be described in terms of a series of 'tragic narratives' which have all failed to solve the central problems of English VET. This history will be described and evaluated through an analysis of policy phases suggested by a number of writers on the topic (Ainley, 1988, 1999; Armitage, *et al.*, 1999; Lea *et al.*, 2003).

## Training for jobs, 1960s–1970s

In response to the relative economic decline as a result of loss of empire and protected markets, the traditional *laissez-faire* approach to VET in England was increasingly challenged in the late 1950s and the 1960s. State intervention was introduced in the form of the 1964 Industrial Training Act which established a Central Training Council (consisting of six employers and six trades union representatives) which advised a regional network of Industrial Training Boards (ITBs) which, by 1966, covered 7.5 million workers (Lees and Chiplin, 1970). Training was financed through a grant/levy system imposed on firms which – though a constant cause of complaint from employers (especially small businesses) – did successfully increase employee training and day-release opportunities for workers throughout the 1960s (Evans, 1992). This was a time of low unemployment and strong trades union power combined with an optimism – fuelled by the then Prime Minister Harold Wilson's reference to forging a 'new Britain in the white heat of the technological revolution' (Armitage *et al.*, 1999, p. 22) – which made clear connections between VET investment and economic growth. Although this period has been characterized by some commentators (Hall, 1994) as merely 'stop gap' or 'gap filling' to remedy short-term skill shortages, there was a genuine belief that the expansion of VET was linked to the expansion of employment and economic growth.

## Training without jobs, 1970s–1980s

The main problems associated with the brief state intervention in training in the 1960s were the lack of success in meeting skilled labour shortages, employer criticisms of ITB financial sanctions, inadequate co-ordination of skills training in different occupations and a failure to provide for the needs of young people in semi-skilled and unskilled jobs (Farley, 1983). In addition to all this, the continuous rise of youth unemployment throughout the period made some form of new initiative imperative. The 1973 Employment and Training Act was meant to deal with these pressing problems by setting up the Manpower Services Commission (MSC) which, formally established in 1974, was intended to bring together all the various elements of the VET and labour market. As Farley (1983) observed:

> The establishment of the MSC marked an important step in linking training with other labour market activities. At the same time it unified, administratively, training services aimed at companies and other employing bodies, with training services aimed at individuals who are unemployed or who want to improve their employment opportunities by acquiring additional skills. (pp. 53–4)

The history of the MSC – from its creation in 1974 to its replacement by the Training Commission, then the short-lived Training Agency which was subsequently superseded by regional Training and Enterprise Councils (TECs) in 1990 – has been described and painstakingly evaluated by Ainley and Corney (1990). The new MSC quango – attacked by industrialists and educators alike, and by politicians of all parties – eventually came to be seen as an 'increasingly sinister corporate creature that was changing the nature of British society – in particular, jobs, training and education' (Benn and Fairley, 1986, p. 12) whose ultimate aim was the 'radical restructuring of the British working class' (Finn, 1986, p. 54). Ainley and Corney (1990) argued that educationalists and teachers

> conceived of the MSC as determined upon narrowing the school curriculum and thus ensuring that the middle class received a standard education whilst the working class was entertained by something called training. (p. 1)

The series of short-lived experiments which marked the MSC's period of power in the 1970s and 1980s – Unified Vocational Preparation, the Youth Opportunities Programmes (YOPs) then Youth Training Schemes (YTS), the Certificate of Pre-Vocational Education (CPVE) and Technical and Vocational Education (TVEI) – have all been fully documented (Finn, 1986; Ainley, 1990; Hyland, 1999) and stand as constant reminders of the grave difficulties standing in the way of VET reform in England. Clearly, injecting increased resources, introducing new programmes and qualifications and new forms of organizing VET is simply not enough to solve the deep-seated problems of a 'low skills–low quality equilibrium' (Finegold and Soskice, 1988) and insufficient demand for high-quality vocational education, particularly when the nature of such problems is constantly transformed by policy changes in response to changing economic and employment conditions.

## New vocationalism, 1980s–1990s

By the early 1980s the MSC was struggling to deal with a number of serious problems in education and training: massive youth unemployment, a low-skilled workforce, and demands from employers for a VET system which met their needs. In addition, a new educational climate had been created by the then Labour Prime Minister James Callaghan's Ruskin College speech in 1976 which had called for an increased emphasis on the economic and vocational function of education at all levels (Hyland, 1994). There was a revival of the perennial employers' complaints that schools were not providing young people with basic skills to equip them for working life. New vocationalism was essentially characterized by pre-vocational schemes – CPVE, YOPs, YTS, TVEI – based on a deficit model which assumed that school-leavers (at least those not studying for A-levels) would typically lack the basic skills necessary for employment. As Armitage *et al.* (1999) argue:

> YTS can be seen as a failure if judged by comparison with earlier vocational training in the narrow sense, and as a pre-vocational scheme. It provided employment for only two-thirds of the trainees who completed the courses and this employment was often short-term. (p. 23)

However, as a number of critical commentators have observed (Ainley, 1988; Lee *et al.*, 1990), such schemes were probably only intended to be stop-gap measures to deal with the urgent problems of massive youth unemployment in the period. As soon as this became less of a problem this strategy was changed, particularly after the Conservative election victory in 1987 when – worried about the growing power of the MSC quango – politicians decided to 'roll back the state' (Evans, 1992, p. 42).

There was a growing realization also at this time that certain levels of both youth and general under/unemployment were endemic and structural. Once the notion of a 'job for life' has been abandoned, different patterns of VET – incorporating recurrent skills training linked to lifelong learning programmes and qualifications – would logically be required.

Another key feature of these years was the growing influence of employers in VET at all levels of the system. In the TECs, YTS and related developments and through the establishment of the National Council for Vocational Qualifications (NCVQ) in 1986 and the subsequent dominance of employer-defined occupational standards with G/NVQs, the idea that employers' roles and needs should have pride of place in VET was gradually accepted by government as being axiomatic. As will be discussed in later chapters, the notion of employer involvement is problematic and, as in the case of employer-dominated programmes and qualifications such as NVQs (dealt with in detail in Chapter 4), needs to be viewed against the historical problems of English VET in which the demands and requirements of employers play a large part. However, the end of the liberal consensus on the aims, nature and purpose of state education, which can be seen as stemming from Callaghan's 1976 speech, can be directly linked to this new vocationalist triumph placing the government's perception of employer and employment needs at the centre of VET design and development.

As Keep (2006) has argued recently, this centralist state control of VET effectively prevents the development of alternative planning and finding systems such as the ones operating in the state partnership models of Continental Europe.

### Education without jobs, 1990s–2000s

This most recent period has witnessed the massive expansion of student numbers in both FE and higher education (HE) alongside a qualification explosion leading to an ever-increasing demand for credentials of all kinds. The two key stated goals of contemporary lifelong learning policy in England are the development of vocational skills for economic competitiveness and the fostering of social inclusion (Hyland, 2003), and the recent expansion of post-school provision might be seen as evidence of the achievement of these goals. However, the persistent problems of VET – particularly the second-class status and low investment in employee development – remain, to be supplemented by potentially new problems linked to lifelong learning and the centralist state planning model operating under New Labour.

Armitage *et al.* (1999) express the problem well in pointing to the fact that although learning and education have come to replace training in many contexts, since all 'mainstream education is dominated by the vocational themes of a work-related, often competence-based curriculum', the whole business has 'become vocationalised in the sense that the connection between the world of work and education is seen as necessary rather than contingent' (pp. 25–6). If we factor into this equation the persistence of the vocational/academic divide, those destined for the second-class route have now, according to a number of recent commentators (Ecclestone, 2004; Hayes, 2003), to experience impoverished vocational programmes dominated by 'therapeutic' objectives linked to fostering personal/social skills and self-esteem in learners rather than traditional knowledge and skills. Hayes (2003) argues that, alongside the 'triumph of vocationalism' over the last few decades, there has been a 'triumph of therapeutic education', a 'form of prescription for work' arising out of the 'changed nexus between work and education' (p. 54). He goes on to explain that:

> The new vocational skills that are required in the workforce are sometimes called 'emotional' or 'aesthetic' labour. If PCET [post-compulsory education and training] students are being trained in personal and social skills as well as in relationships, this is training in emotional labour ... [which] requires and receives a personal and wholehearted commitment to workplace values. (*Ibid.*)

Although this critique is almost certainly far too pessimistic and extreme (see Hyland, 2005), there is a genuine cause for concern in any movement away from a knowledge and skills base in VET to a preoccupation with so-called 'softer' skills such as interpersonal relationships. However, as we will suggest in later chapters, a values dimension of some sort has always been lacking in the vocational route, and the inclusion of some of the objectives eschewed by Hayes and Ecclestone might be just what is required to enhance the status of VET against the background of contemporary lifelong learning policy and practice.

## Apprenticeships – old and new

The idea of apprenticeship – viewed as some sort of teaching/ learning process whereby initiates or novices would be enabled to 'come out of their time' and achieve a form of 'mastery' in a particular field (Parkin, 1978) – goes back to the earliest times when people first organized themselves into recognized communities.

Its central place in both ancient and modern education and training systems may be explained by the necessity of such a process to the crucial vocational functions of transmitting norms and practices vital to survival and reproduction. All societies would have required formal or informal systems in which the young could learn these vital arts and skills, as did the Chellean society of the 'Saber-Tooth Curriculum' mentioned in Chapter 1. Such practices were eventually formalized and systematized as tribes and communities developed religious, puberty and leadership/organizational norms, mores and rituals (Wilds and Lottich, 1970).

Gospel (1998a) has assembled a substantial body of research on apprenticeships and offers a clear account of what might be described as the 'traditional' model which is defined as a

> method of employment and on-the-job training which involves a set of reciprocal rights and duties between an employer and a trainee ... the employer agrees to teach a range of skills, usually of a broad occupational nature; in return, the apprentice agrees to work for an extended period at a training wage which is low compared with the qualified workers' rate. (p. 437)

Having clear links with high levels of craft, skill and mastery (Ainley, 1993), apprenticeship has traditionally played a central role in VET in the UK, and changes in the institution of apprenticeship can be seen to parallel wider social, economic and cultural changes. Emerging from the craft and guilds traditions, medieval apprenticeships reflected the fact that almost all education in the period consisted of 'on-the-job' training based on fixed periods of indenture which, as a general rule, was for seven years between the ages of 14 and 21 (Lawson and Silver, 1978). The system was codified in the Elizabethan period through the 1563 Statute of Artificers which imposed the traditional seven-year indenture on some 30 crafts and, along with the provisions of the 1601 Poor Law, allowed pauper children to become apprentices (Coffey, 1992).

Towards the end of the eighteenth century, apprenticeship came under increasing pressure. A notable attack on the institution appeared in *The Wealth of Nations* by Adam Smith in 1776. In a chapter entitled 'The Policy of Europe' he argued that apprenticeship and the guilds that sustained it were an outmoded form of industrial training and a form of what economists nowadays call 'producer capture', whereby the guilds arranged labour market supply so as to defend their own interests and the craft workers who controlled them. Smith argued that not only was apprenticeship an inefficient mode of training but also that it supported an outdated system of production. The fragmentation of work into small components, each separately requiring little or no skill input, argued Smith, rendered elaborate forms of vocational education unnecessary. Even for the manufacture of watches, he argued, the training of workers for a few weeks and even a few days would suffice (Smith, 1981, Vol. I, Bk I, pp. 139–40). Whatever the direct effect of his arguments, the Statute of Artificers was repealed in 1814. In France guilds were abolished during the Revolution and apprenticeship there has never recovered fully, remaining both a minor form of VET and of relatively low status (Géhin, 2006; Nuffield Foundation, 2005). The decline of craft work and the rise of mass production was to put apprenticeship under further pressure. Thus, by the mid-nineteenth century this traditional form of apprenticeship was being increasingly replaced by 'live-out' arrangements as – largely because of the changing nature of work and social life following the Industrial Revolution – the institution spread to non-artisan trades such as electrical engineering and metalworking.

The decline and dilution of apprenticed trades and occupations continued into the twentieth century as a result of 'modern mass production' (Schofield, 1923, p. 19) and – particularly after the First World War – the tendency of employers to split traditional jobs such as skilled metalworking into constituent parts (reminiscent of the more recent functional analysis methodology of the NCVQ). From the 1920s on, the apprenticeship system was subjected to fierce criticism on the grounds that it:

> Involved unnecessary time-serving [satirized as time-wasting], that it did not train to consistent standards, was not well suited to modern technological occupations, perpetuated outdated and irrelevant demarcations between trades, and was predominantly restricted to young male workers. (Adams, 1996, p. 6)

Many of these criticisms echoed those of Adam Smith made 150 years earlier.

The arguments of critics such as Wilkinson (1931) that 'sitting by Nellie' methods of apprenticeship training should be replaced by more systematic approaches gradually began to influence employers and politicians, particularly after Williams's (1963) large-scale study compared the British system unfavourably with its European counterparts. Key criticisms of British practices – particularly in relation to the German Dual System – concerned both the quality (little external monitoring of training, low day-release participation rates) and the quantity (inflexible five-year training period, rigid divisions between skill areas and skilled/unskilled occupational tasks) of training, and these influenced policy-makers responsible for implementing the 1964 Industrial Training Act. The 1964 Act – which introduced Industrial Training Boards (ITBs) and a grant-levy system on firms to finance VET – did produce a modest expansion of apprenticeships for young men, from 35% to 43% of the age group between 1950 and 1969 (though figures for young women show a slight decline from 8% to 7%; Hyland, 1999, p. 38). However, this grant-levy system was always unpopular with employers and was abolished with the establishment of the MSC in 1973.

Against the background of the de-industrialization of Britain throughout the 1980s, the period of the MSC witnessed a sharp decline in apprenticeships – from 107,400 in 1978 to 34,500 in 1990 (Gospel, 1995, p. 37). Along with employers' perennial complaints about the failure of schooling to prepare youngsters for working life, the decline in apprenticeships fuelled an increasing concern about the erosion of the nation's craft and technician skills base (Finegold, 1999). In response, the then Conservative government – after introducing a number of reforms which de-regulated the training and youth labour market – set about redesigning apprenticeship on the basis, in Rikowski's (1998) words, of 'low youth wage expectation and the dominance of employer interests' (p. 16). The rationale for VET in general and apprenticeship in particular moved away from what Senker (1992) called a 'time-serving concept of training towards an achievement basis' (p. 61), and this paved the way for the development of new models.

The Modern Apprenticeship (MA) programme – announced in 1993 with a three-year budget of £1.25 billion – was established as a prototype in 1994 and launched nationally in 1995. Principal aims of MAs included the provision of employer-based learning for 16 to 25-year-olds to NVQ level 3, the improvement of the supply of intermediate skills (craft, technician and supervisory) to remedy shortages, and the incorporation of 'job-specific, key skills and occupational knowledge' to ensure that the 'Modern Apprenticeship offers both a relevant and flexible structure to the training needs of industry' (Skills and Enterprise Network, 1997, p. 1). Adams (1996, pp. 40–5) has analysed these early MA developments in some detail and offers a useful summary of key differences and similarities between MAs and old apprenticeships.

The principal differences turn on the formalized training plans of the new model aimed at NVQ level 3 as against the less formal aims of the older model, a noticeably larger number of female MAs than the traditional system, and a more flexible approach to time-serving. However, although MAs are theoretically divorced from the fixed periods of indenture characteristic of the old apprenticeships, 'contracts have emerged as a significant feature of MAs despite their redundancy in the traditional apprenticeship' and the 'minimum time period required to obtain an apprenticeship [i.e. reach NVQ level 3] in certain occupations is not significantly different from their predecessors' (*ibid*., p. 41). As Gospel (1998a) notes, the new schemes incorporate 'both traditional and novel features' including a 'written agreement on traditional lines between the employer and apprentice, specifying rights and obligations' (p. 21). He goes on to observe that:

> A crucial part of the Modern Apprenticeship is that the whole of the wage and part of the training costs are borne by the employer. But government also contributes towards the cost of off-the-job training, establishing for the first time in Britain the principle of state support for part-time education and training for employed young people. (*Ibid*.)

Rikowski (1998) comes to similar conclusions in noting that MAs were 'viewed by the DfEE [Department for Education and Employment] as being based on the best of traditional apprenticeships' with periods of training linked to 'dedicated employers'; indeed, in some respects they were 'not unlike post-1964 modern or even classical apprenticeships' (pp. 16–17). Rikowski goes on, however, to make the interesting observation that 'although MAs clearly have links with the past through their attachment to lifelong learning', they can 'best be described as Postmodern apprenticeships' since they 'imply a different approach to both apprenticeship and mastery' (p. 17). Indeed, Rikowski argues that, unlike former models, the new (post-) modern versions linked to lifelong learning imply that there 'is no end point to learning' and that, since such 'learning is incompatible with mastery', postmodern apprentices are 'always going to be subject to the vagaries of rapid technological and labour market changes'. In postmodernized apprenticeship the 'horizon is always just distant . . . it shifts with rapid technological change' (*ibid*., pp. 17–18, 20). Perhaps here Rikowski has a tendency to conflate technological change and so-called never-ending apprenticeship in a potentially confusing way. MAs are time limited, just like classical ones; the problem is that the skills they incorporate may be rapidly outdated (hence the quest for allegedly core or key skills claimed to be generally transferable; see Hyland and Johnson, 1998). It is worth noting that the German approach of teaching principles and underpinning theoretical knowledge – and indeed the 'common foundation of general education or *culture générale* as it is termed in France' (Green, 1997, p. 92) which characterizes the VET systems of France, Japan and Sweden – makes such outdating far less likely.

Early indications for the new MA schemes were promising. By spring 2000, 325,000 16 to 25-year-olds had joined programmes covering 82 industrial sectors (Unwin and Wellington, 2001, p. 13). Moreover, the new models had managed to incorporate new occupational sectors, such as local government and the armed forces, enhanced the basic minimum achievement from level 2 to 3, and encouraged many more young women to undertake apprenticeships. The number of young people leaving the work-based route with level 3 qualifications doubled between 1995 and 2000, and in some regions 'over 90% of those completing their MAs were still in employment after their training – around half of them with the same company that they had trained with' (LSC, 2001a, p. 1).

On the demerit side, a number of problems and shortcomings have emerged. A 1998 Centre for Economic Performance report noted that although the take-up of MAs trebled between 1994 and 1997, they were 'still the post-school choice of only 20% of young people compared to 67% in Germany' (Hart, 1998, p. 27). Similar unfavourable comparisons were cited in the DfEE (2001) response to the National Skills Task Force Final Report in the observation that 'around 4 in 10 of those in jobs in the UK hold the equivalent of A level qualifications or higher, but in Germany the figure is double' and 'among young adults in Japan and Korea more than double' (p. 11). In addition, the relatively low level of completion rates for MAs (i.e. those leaving with level 3 qualifications) was a cause for concern. Typically, completion rates were around 40% in most sectors, ranging from 56% in Construction and 54% in Engineering Manufacture to 16% in Hotel, Catering and Retailing (Unwin and Wellington, 2001, p. 14).

Moreover, Adams (1996) stressed the weaknesses of the original MA links with the 'pseudo-minimalist approach of

NVQs' as opposed to the 'broad based skills acquired by apprentices in traditional occupations' (p. 47), particularly in view of the lifelong learning objective of fostering the so-called multi-skilled and flexible workers said to be required by post-Fordist economies. More worrying still was the problem of providing adequate support, guidance and co-ordination of learning on work-based schemes. A Training Standards Council report noted that 'trainee support services, as a whole, were poorly co-ordinated' (Sherlock, 1999, p. 10), and Unwin and Wellington (2001) concluded that their data showed

> quite vividly that systematic, well-planned mentoring and structured ongoing assessment are not occurring as they should on the modern apprenticeship. Mentoring is dependent upon personal, sometimes chance or fortuitous relationships and meetings – as opposed to carefully planned and monitored mentor-mentee contact time. Assessment is equally ad hoc, depending on the willingness of an employee to interact with an apprentice or the energy and enthusiasm of a young person to 'bother' or 'hassle' a fellow worker. (p. 109)

The reconstruction of MAs in 2001 – involving the establishment of Foundation Modern Apprenticeships (FMAs to replace National Traineeships at level 2) and Advanced Modern Apprenticeships (AMAs to level 3), in addition to Foundation Degrees and Graduate Apprenticeships (DfEE, 2001) – was a direct response to the problems identified in the original MA programme. New Technical Certificates and Diplomas – incorporating key skills and vocational learning wider than basic NVQs – were designed to improve completion rates and strengthen the content of programmes. Improvements in the light of identified weaknesses were also in evidence in the reconstructed MA provisions for 'a national framework for apprenticeship which defines basic standards and strengthens the relationship between the employer and the apprentice' plus an 'entitlement to a Modern Apprenticeship place for all 16 and 17 year olds with five or more passes at grades A to G from 2004' (DfES, 2001, p. 1). The most recent figures indicate that 178,900 young people aged 16–21 started an apprenticeship in

2004/05, and that completion rates had increased by 29% over the previous year (LSC, 2005a).

## Summary and conclusion

The history of VET in England in the twentieth century can be viewed as a series of short-lived and unsatisfactory attempts to reform the system in the light of a number of persistent problems (continuing into the present century with skills strategies and FE policy papers; DfES, 2006a, 2006b) which, at the time of writing, seem to be worsening (Hayward, 2004; Keep, 2006). Progress made in the present millennium will be examined at greater length in the final chapter. Before this, the next chapter examines the experience of other countries in the development of VET.

# 3 'They Do Things Differently Over There': Vocational Education in Europe

## Cultural, social and political differences

In the previous two chapters we have seen how British culture has shaped British vocational education. Britain is no exception to other countries in this respect; vocational education tends to be, to a large extent, not just a response to economic need but also an expression of a country's culture and values. This partly explains the British tendency to place a lot of value on liberal education and to make a sharp distinction between liberal and vocational education. There are important factors that have, historically, interacted with each other. First, the gentlemanly ideal of liberal education, derived from Greek thought and society, persisted into the industrial period. Second, Britain, as the birthplace of liberal economics, developed a particular industrial structure and workplace hierarchy during the eighteenth and nineteenth centuries. This latter development was connected with earlier events in English history, notably the creation of a landless and rootless 'reserve army of labour' due to the enclosure of common land. This movement accelerated the decline of the medieval occupational guilds and apprenticeships, and the Industrial Revolution undermined these still further. On the other hand, one important European country (France) had a political revolution that consciously swept away medieval institutions and built upon an already strong, centralized state to develop a national system of vocational education. To take yet another example, a country which came late to statehood (Germany) was able to preserve and develop important elements of its medieval social and economic structure into the period which succeeded the initial Industrial Revolution. These tensions and anomalies are explored in painstaking detail by Green (1990) who concludes that while economic, social, cultural and political factors all had a part to play in the establishment of compulsory state schooling from the beginning of the nineteenth century, it was the peculiar requirements of the nation-state itself and the needs of state-building which primarily drove educational developments in Germany, France, England and the USA.

England developed a 'hybrid' VET system based partly on the remains of apprenticeship, partly on Mechanics Institutes and Technical Colleges, and partly on contingent 'on-the-job' training. The school system has never, until very recently, played a significant part in VET (but see Sanderson 1994 on the Junior Technical Schools of the first half of the twentieth century). France has developed a school-based, centralized VET system (Géhin, 2006) and Germany, a collaborative arrangement between work-based apprenticeship and a broader education in vocational colleges (Greinert, 2006). These developments arose from the history of the respective countries, and also represent deeply rooted features of their societies. There is an important message here: the way in which vocational education develops concerns not just the technical solution to an economic need but the way in which a society preserves and develops its cultural and moral heritage.

## Different models of VET: workplace-based, school-based and hybrid

We have chosen England, France and Germany as main comparisons because each, in its own way, represents significantly different ways of conducting vocational education. They do not exhaust the possibilities and there are all kinds of hybrid systems (such as the Netherlands; Westerhuis, 2006), but each of them represents a different model.

Let us first look at workplace-based systems. Historically, the most important of these has been *apprenticeship*. Traditionally, apprenticeship involves the adoption of a young person as employee, paid at low rate, often supported by a fee from parents. In return the young person is inducted into the knowledge necessary to practise the employer's occupation and comes to participate in the tradition and way of life associated with that occupation. Since the young person is not initially very economically productive, the employer incurs a cost in taking him or her on. Only later does the value generated by the employee contribute to profits. Until that time the apprentice is paid less than an accredited worker or 'journeyman' (Foreman-Peck, 2004). In the Middle Ages, this system of vocational training was associated with trade corporations or guilds, which controlled what we would now call industrial sectors, including entry and training requirements. The guild system was particularly associated with *craft* production, or the use of technique by a workman to produce a finished article, usually, but not necessarily, without theoretical education.

Apprenticeship declined for a variety of reasons, which varied from country to country. In some cases, such as France, political revolution resulted in the deliberate uprooting of medieval institutions, of which the guilds and their associated vocational education through apprenticeship were one (Géhin, 2006). The second was the decline of craft production and its replacement by mass production and scientifically based technique, for example in England (Marx, 1887/1970). Finally, there was an ideological polemic against the guild system associated with the eighteenth-century economist, Adam Smith (1776) which resulted in a weakening of the legislative framework underpinning traditional apprenticeship in Britain. It is important, however, to remember that apprenticeship, although traditionally associated with trade guilds, is not necessarily bound to them and continues to this day as a small but significant element in vocational education (Ainley and Rainbird, 1999; Gospel and Fuller, 1998; Ryan, 2004). Britain, for example, still manages to retain a small but significant amount of apprenticeship in its overall mix of vocational education.

There is, however, an important group of countries that modernized their apprenticeship system to take account of the new industrial realities of the twentieth century. These countries include Germany, Austria and Switzerland (Green *et al.*, 1999). In order to understand this development it is necessary to understand how Germany responded to American methods of mass industrial production. At the beginning of the twentieth century industrial firms, such as Siemens, reorganized production to take account of the method described by Smith and Marx and developed on a large scale in the United States, which is commonly known as the *division of labour*, but which would be better described as a *fragmentation of the labour process* (Williams, 2000). Instead of a single craft worker taking responsibility for the whole of the process of manufacture, the whole process is organized managerially and separate tasks are delegated in a sequence to individual workers. This is described at the beginning of Adam Smith's *Wealth of Nations* (1776/ 1981) using pin-making as an example and he claims that production organized in such a way leads to greatly increased individual productivity per hour. The corollary of Smith's account is that the skill of the craftsman is dissipated and instead rests with the inventor, the technologist and the manager. The individual worker becomes deskilled and requires little or no vocational education or even on-the-job training. In order to avoid becoming a complete moron, however, he is going to need a basic education, part funded by the state, and this will also render him less susceptible to revolutionary demagogy (*ibid.*, Vol. II, Bk V).

German industry did not accept this corollary of mass production. Firms like Siemens used the division of labour and largely abolished craft production within their factories. They did not, however, deskill their workforce. They adapted the American system of mass production to the kind of economic strategy for which Germany has become renowned, namely high-quality, high-specification production, sometimes known as 'flexible specialisation' and sometimes as 'diversified quality production' (Streeck, 1992). They accepted the principle of the industrial division of labour superseding traditional craft production, but maintained skilled input into the processes that made up the totality of production. This approach also involved a degree of scientific understanding of the principles underlying production (Hanf, 2006). This compromise has underpinned German industrial production ever since.

Germany's response to the Industrial Revolution did, however, lead to a new model of vocational education. This was due in large part to the work of a Bavarian educationist, Georg

Kerschensteiner (1854–1932), who was director of the Munich education system for a crucial period. Kerschensteiner was, in many ways, a progressive educator in the Pestalozzian tradition, but he also believed, like Aristotle, in a form of moral education that involved development of the virtues. Crucially, he was convinced that vocational education should be education in the broadest sense, including character and civic development, scientific and liberal elements (Winch, 2006). It was not possible or desirable to cover all these within the traditional apprenticeship. The academic element of education could not be covered satisfactorily and neither could the demands of citizenship in a modern society moving towards democratic governance. Kerschensteiner's solution in Munich was to increase the practical element in school education in the *Volksschule* or elementary school (up to the age of 14) and to develop a mandatory element of college education for apprentices, which took the form of release for a couple of days a week. Thus was developed the *Berufschule* or vocational college, which worked in concert with the workplace to develop an integrated vocational education for apprentices between the ages of 14 and 20. Germany came to adopt this system countrywide and, although education is compulsory up to the age of 15, most young Germans continue their education within the *Dual System*, which is the integrated workplace-college model just described. This approach has also been adopted by Austria, Switzerland and Denmark.

Europe is, however, nothing if not diverse, and the Dual System is only one of a number of approaches adopted by European countries. One other significant approach is that adopted most notably by France, which is to base the main part of initial vocational education within the school system. By 'school-based system' we understand VET that assumes that those being educated are *students* rather than *employees* as in apprenticeship systems. Thus 'school' can either mean a secondary institution that has a compulsory upper secondary component as well as a lower secondary compulsory programme, *or* it can mean a specialist post-compulsory upper secondary sector which also incorporates some other post-compulsory educational activity. In other words, what we call

'Further Education Colleges' are components of a school-based system in this sense. It is important to realize that school-based systems do not exclude part-time (day or block release) workplace experience, just as apprenticeship does not exclude part-time attendance at a college. Students thus *alternate* between the academic institution and the workplace, but crucially, unlike apprenticeship, the student is not an employee with the rights and duties of an employee. The advantages of colleges is that they can employ staff with commercial and industrial experience, as well as using specialist buildings and equipment that are designed for the occupations which the students hope to enter. France, before the French Revolution, used apprenticeship but, as mentioned above, it was greatly damaged, and deliberately so, by the revolutionary governments (Géhin, 2006), although it continues as a small but significant element in French VET (Green et al., 1999, p. 185). In subsequent years, the state developed specialist vocational schools especially for technologists as opposed to technicians (Green, 1990) and, more recently, school-based vocational education has become a significant responsibility of the upper secondary school system as mass upper secondary education has developed. Other countries have also adopted a predominantly school-based route, for example the Netherlands, Belgium, Sweden and Spain (Green et al., 1999). The United States is yet another country that relies heavily on a school-based system and on vocational tracking within the compulsory secondary education sector (Lewis, 2006), together with post-compulsory college-based education. Britain retains apprenticeship but relies heavily on vocational courses in secondary schools and further education colleges, and so is predominantly a school-based system in this sense. However, the Modern Apprenticeship, since it is subsidized by the state, is not, in the strict sense, an apprenticeship system.

So much for institutional variety. What exactly are the social, political and cultural differences that underpin these different systems? Britain represents a society in which there has traditionally been a sharp distinction between liberal and vocational education, which has been maintained in aims, curricula and institutions up to and including the present day. But we should be wary of exaggerating this divide and also of thinking that it does not exist in other countries (as it does). The issue, though, is not so much about whether or not vocational and liberal education enjoy 'parity of esteem' (they do not in almost any country), but whether or not vocational education enjoys some esteem and, if so, how much and in what respect. Here, cross-national differences are interesting and instructive.

Germany has a strong and distinctive tradition of liberal education, usually described using the term 'Bildung'. However, *Bildung* is a much more complex concept than liberal education as it is understood in Britain and, in important respects, departs significantly from it. In the first place *Bildung* is only partly to be understood as preparation for life; it includes school- and college-based liberal education (*Allgemeinbildung*) but it nevertheless remains essentially incomplete, as it encompasses personal development in the widest sense during the course of life, including in the workplace. This extended idea of *Bildung* was referred to by Wilhelm von Humboldt as '*allgemeine Menschenbildung*' or general human education, and early educational experiences were its essential preliminary rather than its culmination. It is important to realize that there is a significant German tradition of seeing some of the liberal aims of education taking place through sustained occupational engagement, resulting in a process of self-discovery and the adoption of personal values. This can be clearly seen in the *Bildungsroman* or 'novel of Bildung' tradition exemplified in authors such as Goethe and Keller. In these stories a young man goes into the world under the influence of an occupational engagement and seeks to understand whether that occupation is one that suits him and, in the course of doing so, finds out important truths about himself. The idea is that the occupation (acting in the case of Goethe's Wilhelm Meister, painting in Keller's Heinrich Lee) is a part of life and the hero must establish whether he is up to the demands of such a life and what the search for excellence in an occupational field tells him about himself.

In Humboldt's conception of universal education, school-based education was the basis for vocational education, which could be accessed at any point after the primary phase, largely depending on one's social class background. But school and vocational education (usually through an apprenticeship) were just the first, but necessary, phases of *allgemeine Menschenbildung*, which was a lifetime process (Benner, 2003). This Humboldtian conception of *Bildung* has a superficial resemblance to what we now call 'lifelong learning'. However, there are important differences: 'lifelong learning' is geared to the idea that one needs to change jobs and to be able to learn in order to be adaptable to different kinds of workplaces. By contrast, countries that maintain strong occupational identities, such as Germany, see the occupation as a lifetime commitment, but also hold that one develops *within* the occupation, both through taking further occupational qualifications, such as becoming a *Meister* or senior operative capable of educating others within the occupation, but also through the experiences of taking responsibility and working with others. These aspirations for vocational education are well represented in the 'competences' which German trainees are expected to master and which are inscribed in the regulations for the different recognized occupations (*Berufe*).

These 'competences' are of three kinds. First, there is the technical side of occupational ability or 'Fachkompetenz', which consists of 'the inclination and ability, based on excellent knowledge and know-how, to solve problems by the right methods, with decisiveness, appropriate means and autonomously'. Then there are the personal competences, which consist of the 'inclination and ability to clarify, test and judge, to develop opportunities, to take into account demands and restrictions set by family, occupation and the public, to fulfil one's own potential and to form and develop one's own life plans.' The personal competences include qualities such as 'autonomy, a critical faculty, self-confidence, reliability, a sense of responsibility and duty and, in particular, the development of moral concepts and self-chosen commitment to moral values.' Finally, there are the social competences, which include 'the inclination and ability to experience and form social relationships, to realise and understand loyalty, to understand and to engage with other people rationally and responsibly, to develop social responsibility and solidarity' (BIBB, 2005).

It should be evident from these specifications that 'Ausbildung' or vocational education in the Dual System, especially in Germany, is a much broader concept than industrial training and includes significant elements of personal development. The language of 'competences' will be all too familiar to British vocational educators and points to one of the problems of understanding vocational education, namely the complex, ambiguous and shifting language that is used to describe vocational knowledge and understanding in their broadest senses. The term 'competence', as it was introduced into the British context, was done so in a deliberate way so as to align vocational knowledge with narrowly specified behaviours (Hyland, 1993). This narrow idea of competence underlies the NVQ conception of vocational ability, well expressed in Jessup's (1991) remark that: 'Skills can only be demonstrated through their application in performance (doing something) while knowledge can be elicited through the more abstract means of conversation, questioning or working' (p. 121). A major problem with statements like this is that they conflate behaviour with action, and quite incorrectly suggest that action does not require underlying knowledge. People do not just exhibit 'behaviour' like boulders rolling down a hill; they *act* in order to achieve certain goals, often in concert with other people and in the light of values that they identify with. A narrow, behaviourally specified idea of competence in terms of performance on a specific task fails to capture most of what is important about action in vocational contexts (these issues are explored in more detail in Chapter 4).

A close look at the German occupational competences, however, suggests that the term is misused in Germany in a different way. Here we see explicit reference to underpinning knowledge, to social interaction, to the world outside the immediate workplace, and to autonomy, responsibility and virtues such as loyalty and reliability. Just as it is misleading to narrow down action to behaviour, so it is misleading to describe as 'competences' what are clearly forms of knowledge, personal qualities and virtues. Here we come across one of the central problems of understanding developments in vocational education, namely the confusing use of terminology that obscures underlying concepts. 'Competence' sounds much harder and more commercial than 'old-fashioned' terms like 'knowledge', 'character' and 'virtue', but the undiscriminating terminology does not clarify the situation, but rather confuses it.

This becomes much clearer once we look at the sources of the German idea of occupational competence. We have already seen that *Bildung* in its broadest sense has traditionally had a perfectly respectable association with occupational engagement. The origins of the Dual System, however, as we have just seen, lie in the work of Georg Kerschensteiner and his philosophy of vocational education. The model of vocational education that he developed in Munich was to become a national and, indeed to some extent, an international one. To understand Kerschensteiner, it is vital to realize that he was at least as much concerned with the personal development of young people as he was with economic development. Indeed he explicitly states that the aim of vocational education should be *Bildung* and that this involves an engagement with 'timeless values' (Kerschensteiner, 1925/1968).

Kerschensteiner believed, following Pestalozzi, that people learn best in practical situations. One of the problems with schools is that they fail to provide a sufficient number of situations of that kind. This makes them, in a sense, problematic as learning environments. By 'practical situations' Kerschensteiner does not just mean situations where one has an opportunity for manual or corporeal activity, but where what one might call 'operational conditions' apply. In other words, Kerschensteiner is more concerned with 'real-life' conditions where the standard of one's work matters, where time is critical, where other people depend on one's own abilities and judgement and where mistakes may have serious consequences. Only in such situations will young people develop qualities of character such as commitment, perseverance and self-discipline. Schooling could provide such situations only in an imperfect way through the provision of workshops, and sporting and outdoor activities. However, providing them even in an imperfect state is better than not providing them at all.

On the other hand, the workplace also had its drawbacks as an educational location. In the workplace, the young worker could develop the 'bourgeois virtues' such as diligence, self-mastery, persistence and attention to detail. These, Kerschensteiner thought, were all very well as far as they went, but they did not go far enough in providing for *Bildung*. In particular, the workplace in itself was not properly equipped to develop the 'civic virtues' such as loyalty, considerateness, autonomy and civic pride. But workplaces also held a couple of significant dangers. One problem was that young workers could become so fixated on producing for money that they lost sight of the broader personal significance of what they were doing. Another danger was that, in their fixation with getting the product right through exclusive exercise of the 'bourgeois virtues', they would neglect their workmates and the broader consequences for society of their work activity. A young worker might become an excellent, though narrowly focused, craftsman through a traditional apprenticeship, but this would not be enough to turn him into a citizen and a rounded human being. Kerschensteiner's solution to the problem of the inadequacies of school and workplace as educational situations was to combine what he saw as the best features of both. The remarkable success of his proposals is due in part to their location in German educational traditions and partly to do with their relevance to the second wave of industrialization in the latter part of the nineteenth century, in which Germany played a significant role.

Kerschensteiner was dissatisfied with a number of aspects of the apprenticeship that he saw in Munich firms. First, they often provided limited opportunity for broader skill development. Second, they were not really capable of providing young workers with an adequate theoretical grounding in their disciplines. Third, they did not provide safe environments in which to practise skills. Finally, they were unable to provide general, moral or civic education. So while Kerschensteiner's solution for the compulsory lower secondary school was to develop practical, work-related activities, his solution for post-compulsory (and later, post-school compulsory) education was to provide mandatory college day-release for apprentices in which the four elements of their education that could not adequately be developed in the workplace would be catered for. The distinctive feature of the Dual System is that it takes the young person as employee, but gives him or her an extended technical, general and civic education as well as a specialized occupationally based vocational education.

The Dual System has been remarkably successful for a number of reasons. First, it fitted well with the system of industrial training set up by Siemens and other firms at the end of the nineteenth century, which required functionally specialized, but skilled and adaptable workers. Second, this industrial model drew on and adapted a craft tradition on which Kerschensteiner's ideas about vocational education as a form of apprenticeship were based. Third, the model of 'flexible specialisation', to which the Dual System is attuned, formed the basis of Germany's competitive advantage as a high-specification manufacturer. The model was also adaptable to the service sector, where the relative autonomy and adaptability of flexibly trained workers promoted efficiency (Prais *et al.*, 1989). Fourth, the college-workplace model was well placed to develop workers with practical knowledge which involved the application of theory to practice, thus moving the craft worker into the position of technical worker, using science and technology in new industrial and economic processes. Finally, the Dual System enabled extended academic and civic education to take place alongside vocational training, thus promoting the place of industrial workers as a key and respected part of the society. Although vocational education does not enjoy 'parity of esteem' with academic education, it does still enjoy considerable esteem, not only for its quality, but because, through regulation of the labour market through licence to practise, it provides the gateway to respected and well-paid employment.

## Key features of vocational education in Europe

We have devoted much space to the Dual System because it is such an important and distinctive model of vocational education. But the school-based systems of France, the Netherlands, Belgium and Scandinavia also represent a tradition of vocational education that is different from that of the UK and the Mediterranean countries such as Spain, Italy and Greece, in the sense that most young people go through higher secondary education either on a vocational or non-vocational track, rather than entering the labour market at age 16. Those that take a vocational route through secondary education then usually go on to further job-specific training within the workplace. The key point about these countries and their economies is that they assume a relatively highly educated workforce that has acquired a general vocational education which is, in some cases, what Stanton (2004) calls 'strongly vocational'. A 'strongly vocational' education, while not necessarily preparing someone for a specific job, nevertheless aims to develop skills and attitudes appropriate to occupations through the use of material and equipment to be found in the workplace, under the tutelage of teachers with occupational experience of their own.

The mass nature of school-based vocational education provides a level of knowledge and skill which enables more specific and more advanced skills to be built on workplace-based learning. In addition, the closure of the labour market to adolescents prevents the option for employers of the large-scale employment of unskilled labour. Instead, employers are required to make use of the relatively well-developed abilities of the great majority of entrees onto the labour market who have received some form of extended school-based vocational education. Such forms of initial vocational education are associated with 'high-skill equilibrium' economies which rely on a highly trained, highly skilled workforce to buy relatively expensive high-specification, high-quality goods (Finegold, 1991). Like the German system, these school-based systems often involve a significant amount of academic education related to the occupation, together with civic and general education (Clarke and Wall, 2000). Those countries like the UK, which have an unregulated labour market which allows the early entry of unskilled employees, are thought to have the contrary attributes of high dependency on poorly trained, low-paid employees buying low-specification, low-quality goods at low prices (Ashton and Green, 1996). Such economies have lower levels of participation in post-compulsory vocational education, usually have unregulated youth labour markets and rely heavily on contingent, job-specific, firm-based vocational education. They may also, as in the UK, produce young people with qualifications which do not necessarily match employer needs, so necessitating labour market entry into sectors that require low levels of occupation-specific qualifications (Hayward, 2004). A key difference between England and the USA and the Northern European Systems is that the former have a *laissez-faire* 'voluntarist' and employer-centred focus, while, to a greater or lesser degree, countries like France and Germany operate forms of 'social partnership', whereby VET is organized and run through a process of negotiation between trade unions and employers, mediated by the state.

## The United States: tracking in the high school

The United States is an example of a country that has a long tradition of school-based 'strongly vocational' education. Despite the influence of John Dewey, who advocated what could be called relatively weakly vocational forms of practically based education in the secondary school, the influence of David Snedden, who advocated job-specific industrial training geared to the needs of employers, prevailed at the beginning of the twentieth century. Snedden's influence had a profound influence within the school system leading to *tracking*, whereby pupils followed vocational, rather than academic, streams within the high school. In practice such vocational tracks were broadly exclusive of the more academic ones and were largely monopolized by ethnic minorities and poorer people, giving rise to justified concerns among educators about the equity and social wisdom of such a segregated approach (Lewis, 2006). Like the UK, the USA has a largely unregulated labour market and has traditionally relied on importing much of its requirements for skilled labour, rather than training it domestically (Waks, 2004). However, it has a dual track approach to skills, operating in both the high- and the low-skill equilibrium mode (Ashton and Green, 1996). It thus has a very extensive system of vocationally oriented tertiary-level education offering qualifications from our equivalent of Higher National Certificate/ Diploma (HNC/D) upwards which caters both for specialized labour and for generic managers.

# Conclusion

This very brief survey of some other countries' VET systems suggests that each country draws on its own specific social, political and cultural background and values, as well as on its preferred method of economic development, to construct its own conception of vocational education. These national features are particularly evident at initial level, where the general education of the young person still plays a significant role, often within an extended compulsory phase of secondary education. However, as well as national traditions, one can also discern broad models of approach to VET, encompassing some form of post-apprenticeship, school-based (in the broad sense of 'school') and contingent 'on-the-job' training. The Dual System stands out as having a well-argued philosophical base and represents an attempt to adapt the essentially medieval institution of apprenticeship to the industrial and post-industrial age. It will be interesting to see how the Dual System manages to cope with globalization and 'fast capitalism' and the competition from low-wage economies with relatively high levels of education, although it is worth noting that all systems associated with a high-skill equilibrium may come under pressure from societies such as India and China, which are able to combine high-skill production with a very low labour cost base. However, it would be premature for the low-cost, low-skill economies and VET systems of countries such as Italy, Britain and the USA to gloat, since they are likely, *a fortiori*, to be out-competed by low-skill, low-cost production in these countries anyway. The challenge for VET in Europe and the USA is also a challenge for the economies of these countries, namely how to find a place in a world where their competitive advantages are under constant threat of erosion.

# 4 'Competence is All': Behaviourist Reductionism in the English VET Curriculum: The Rise of Skill-talk and Competence-based Education and Training

## Skills and vocationalism

The early chapters outlining the different phases of development of VET in England pointed to the emergence of a reinterpretation of the aims and content of education which paralleled the vocationalization of educational processes from the 1970s onwards. From the activities of the MSC running through the YTS programmes and the new vocationalist initiatives of this period, the educational enterprise as a whole – alongside the increasing merger of education and training – came to be defined in terms of skills and later (following the establishment of the NCVQ in 1986) competences. By the late 1970s, Hart (1978) was noting that 'you cannot dip much into educational writings without realising that the ambit of so-called "skills" is growing' (p. 205), and a decade later commentators were observing that 'the word "skill" is ubiquitous in contemporary educational discourse' (Barrow, 1987, p. 188) to the extent that 'skills are now officially seen as an essential part of the curriculum' (Griffiths, 1987, p. 203).

Although there are contexts in which the concept of 'skill' is clearly relevant and applicable (Ainley, 1993), there are three main reasons for objecting to its wholesale and undiscriminating use to describe the outcomes of education and training.

1) It is neither a well-founded nor clearly articulated notion, and there is no consensus of understanding about whether it applies to the cognitive, affective or psycho-motor

dimensions of human activity. The term is used 'indiscriminately of what are at best very different types of skill' (Barrow, 1987, p. 188). All the following are examples of essential 'skills' recommended in educational literature over the last few decades:

a)  file or sort things, fill in a record book or manual, cutting with one blade (FEU, 1982); taking orders, making conversation (MSC, 1977); writing legibly (DES, 1985);

b)  communication, problem-solving, numeracy, information technology (NCC, 1990); planning, fault-finding, making comparisons (Annett and Sparrow, 1985);

c)  working with others, improving one's own learning and performance (NCVQ, 1992); considering others' views (DES, 1985); human relationship skills (Nelson-Jones, 1989); enterprise skills (TA, 1990).

As Jonathan (1987) has argued, when faced with lists which include 'life skills, reasoning skills, survival skills, etc.' (p. 93), we are bound to ask questions about whether the same concept of skill is being used in all cases and, indeed, whether the concept can bear the weight of all these diverse interpretations. A common error here seems to involve the invalid move of identifying features common to *different* skills and, from this, inferring the existence of a common *skill*. As Dearden (1984) observes in this respect:

> there may indeed be features common to all skilled performances in virtue of which we call them skilled, but it does not follow from this that it is the *same* skill which is present in each case: in the skater, the juggler, the flautist, the chess player and the linguist. (p. 78, original emphasis).

Moreover, if relatively low-level activities such as 'taking orders' are to be labelled as skills alongside 'improving one's own performance' and 'considering others' views', it is not obvious how the identification of such diverse accomplishments as skills adds anything at all to the basic description of content or procedures. Clearly, items in list (a) above are simply discrete occupational tasks, list (b) items might be more properly described as core learning activities, whereas type (c) items are, arguably, not skills at all but values, attitudes and dispositions.

2) A second objection to the indiscriminate use of skill-talk is that (like the competence movement) it belittles the role of knowledge and understanding in education and training thereby seriously impoverishing all forms of learning. Moreover, the downgrading of knowledge is common to both the skills and the competence literature and both have their origins and rationale in behaviourist psychology (Hyland, 1994). As Jessup (1991) claimed in his justification of the NCVQ approach, the primary concern is not with knowledge, understanding or even learning but with evidence of competent performance, with identifying 'what people need in their heads to perform effectively with their hands, feet, voice, eyes, and so on' (p. 121). Furthermore, there is 'no justification for assessing knowledge for its own sake but only for its contribution to competent performance' (*ibid.*, p. 123). Similarly, Elliott (1993), in his critique of such approaches in teacher education, notes that the behaviourist foundations mean that 'the significance of theoretical knowledge in training is a purely technical or instrumental one' by which knowledge 'belongs to the realm of inputs rather than outputs' and 'can only be justified if it is a necessary condition for generating the desired behavioural outcomes of learning' (p. 17).

Skill-talk displays the same attachment to that view of knowledge revealed in Bloom's (1956) taxonomy of educational objectives which is criticized by Wilson (1972) for its obsession with the idea that 'knowledge is like a physical object which can be broken down or built up into a hierarchy of component parts' (p. 106). This distorted perspective not only mistakenly divorces the theoretical from the practical but also implies that some basic tasks – such as filing, stacking shelves or answering the telephone – require very little knowledge whereas, for example, management or planning activities might require a foundation of high-level or advanced knowledge.

In arguing against attempts by Bloom and others to construct hierarchies which separate factual knowledge from comprehension and application, Gribble (1969) demonstrates how satisfying the full conditions of knowledge for even basic propositions involves quite complex conceptual understanding. He explains that:

> Knowing something involves judging that something is so, and judgement is a complex mental operation. Mental abilities and skills are not separate from knowing something for we are unable to specify mental abilities and skills independently of the various forms of knowledge. (p. 58)

Skills and competences require a foundation of knowledge and understanding, just as education requires an infrastructure of training which can lead 'to the confident deployment of skill and technique in a wide variety of situations' (Winch, 1995, p. 324).

In this respect it is interesting how the paradigm example of the driving test which used to be offered by competence proponents to illustrate the importance in VET of 'what people can do rather than what they know' (UDACE, 1989, p. 6) was conveniently dropped when this was supplemented by a written test of knowledge of the highway code! In a similar vein, Holland (1980) suggests that:

> In wrestling with the problems that are important in a field of study, ideas not skills are what count; and the problems get solved, or transformed, or bypassed, by the person with the profounder conception. (p. 23)

Thus, an over-emphasis on skills might easily lead to a descent into the impracticable since those who possess only techniques or knacks do not fully understand the basis of practice. Such an epistemologically shallow conception of skills flies in the face of current conceptions of lifelong learning and the knowledge requirements of a post-Fordist economy.

3) A further problem with current skill-talk is that skills are thought of as morally neutral attributes rather like the functions of a mechanism. Skills, however, have a moral dimension, both in their actual exercise and in the broader implications of their employment. This is why, as we saw in Chapter 3, in some countries' VET systems, the moral dimension of the exercise of skill is given due acknowledgement. This is, unfortunately, not the case in the UK.

However, notwithstanding this nebulous logical, moral and epistemological status, the rise of skill-talk – from the so-called 'skills revolution' of the 1980s (CBI, 1989) to the more recent work of the government's 'Skills Task Force' (DfEE, 2000b) – has been relentless, culminating in the highly symbolic change of identity at the highest level as the former Department for Education and Employment became the Department for Education and Skills in 2001. This was paralleled by the establishment of the Learning and Skills Council (LSC, 2001a) in the same year to oversee the funding and organization of all post-school education and training except that undertaken in higher education institutions. The skills mania – based partly on wildly mistaken ideas about the transferability of core or key skills (Hyland and Johnson, 1998) – shows no signs of abating, as discussions about skill deficits, gaps and shortages are supplemented by 'skills for life' and 'multi-skills' for a knowledge-driven economy in the ever-expanding firmament of skill-talk. The most recent government document – unifying the goals of and endorsed by the four government departments of the DfES, the Department of Trade and Industry, the Treasury and the Department for Work and Pensions (TSO, 2003) – outlines a 'skills challenge' which is intended to cover all aspects of education, vocational training, the economy, employment and the social life of the nation. In light of our critique of skill-talk, we would have to conclude that far too heavy a burden is being placed on an extremely lightweight, ill-defined and educationally vacuous conception of the abilities required at work and hence of the whole VET enterprise. The notion of a 'skill', as it is used in too many reports and official documents, is far too impoverished to bear the enormous weight that has been put on it.

# Competence-based education and training

The story of how competence-based education and training (CBET) was introduced into VET in England through the establishment of the NCVQ in 1986 has been told by many commentators in the field (Bees and Swords, 1990; Burke, 1995; Bates, 1998; Hyland, 1994). The foundations for a major overhaul of VET were established with the publication of *A New Training Initiative* (DOE, 1981) by the then Department of Employment, though this itself can be viewed as a continuation of MSC strategies introduced with YTS programmes. From the very start, accountability in terms of 'outputs ... the standards that need to be achieved at the end of the learning programme' (Jessup, 1990, p. 18) was predominant. There was an insistence that 'at the heart of the initiative lie standards of a new kind' (DOE, 1981, p. 6), and it was the pursuit of such standards – based on competence outputs constructed through the functional analysis methodology of CBET – which was to provide the driving force for the development of NVQs.

Following the publication of the White Paper *Working Together – Education and Training* (DOE/DES, 1986), the NCVQ was established with a remit to design and implement a new national framework of vocational qualifications with the aim of securing national standards of vocational competence throughout all occupational sectors. From the outset, the key aims of the NCVQ were to 'improve vocational qualifications by basing them on standards of competence required in employment' and to 'establish a National Vocational Qualification (NVQ) framework which is comprehensible and comprehensive and facilitates access, progression and continued learning' (NCVQ, 1989, p. 2). The NCVQ was not itself an awarding body but undertook to accredit or hallmark qualifications awarded by other bodies such as City and Guilds, the Royal Society of Arts (RSA) and the Business and Technology Education Council (BTEC) insisting that it would 'only accredit qualifications which met employment needs' (*ibid.*, p. 3).

National Vocational Qualifications (NVQs) were designed to be a new kind of qualification that was meant to accredit workplace skills, whether or not they resulted from a formal curriculum or process of instruction. Accreditation was to be given on the basis of successful performance in the workplace. All NVQs had to consist of 'an agreed statement of competence, which should be determined or endorsed by a lead body with responsibility for defining, maintaining and improving national standards of performance in the sectors of employment where the competence is practised' (NCVQ, 1991, p. 1). Eleven occupational sectors were identified and these generated over 180 lead bodies. The agreed statement of competence in each occupational sphere 'should be derived from an analysis of the functions within the area of competence to which it relates' and had to be linked to 'performance criteria' which 'identify only the essential aspects of performance necessary for competence', in addition to 'range statements' which 'express the various circumstances in which the competence must be applied' (*ibid.*, pp. 2–3).

This process of functional analysis, used by lead bodies to determine competence, involved the identification of the 'expectations in employment as a whole ... breaking the work role for a particular area into purposes and functions' (Mitchell, 1989, p. 58). The end result was the identification of 'key purposes' for all the various occupational sectors, accompanied by 'units and elements' linked to relevant performance criteria and range statements (see Figure 4.1).

In addition to all this, there was a precisely defined hierarchy of five levels of competence (see Figure 4.2), from basic, routine tasks at level 1 to advanced management and supervisory functions at level 5.

After the NCVQ framework was given official government endorsement as a model for future education and training

UNIT: RECEPTION
ELEMENTS:
01 receive and direct visitors
*Notes*:
Underpinning skills and knowledge: structure, location and responsibilities of people in organisation; policy and procedures of organisation on greeting visitors, security, safety and emergency; messaging procedure; telephone system and operation; effective use of information sources; dealing with difficult/aggressive visitors (e.g. recognise and react appropriately to physical communication signals); car parking arrangements available to visitors; effective communication (oral and written)
*Range*:
Routine and non-routine visitors must be dealt with. Contingencies must be dealt with: callers without appointment (with both urgent and non-urgent requirements), callers who are late/early for appointments, callers who require baggage or other effects to be cared for during visit, receipt of deliveries, emergency situations
*Performance Criteria*:
1. All visitors are greeted promptly and courteously.
2. Visitors' names and needs are identified.
3. Visitors are only given disclosable information.
4. Visitors are directed and/or escorted in accordance with organisation policy.
5. Reasons for any delay/non-availability are explained politely.
6. All records are up to date, legible and accurate.
7. Messages are accurately recorded and passed on promptly to correct location.
8. Security and safety procedures are followed at all times.

**Fig. 4.1:** Example of NVQ units and elements
(*Source*: Hyland, 1994, p. 7)

reform in the 1991 White Paper *Education and Training for the 21st Century* (DES, 1991), there was an increasing tendency – now codified in all official statements about qualifications pathways and levels – to use the five NCVQ levels to indicate some kind of equivalence between NVQs and other vocational and academic qualifications. This resulted in the three-track system – with the broad vocationalism of general NVQs (GNVQs) introduced in 1992 forming a middle track – illustrated in Figure 4.3.

The following definitions of the NVQ levels provide a general guide and are not intended to be prescriptive.

*Level 1*: competence in the performance of a range of varied work activities, most of which may be routine and predictable.

*Level 2*: competence in a significant range of varied work activities, performed in a variety of contexts. Some of the activities are complex and non-routine, and there is some individual responsibility or autonomy. Collaboration with others, perhaps through membership of a work group or team, may often be a requirement.

*Level 3*: competence in a broad range of varied work activities performed in a wide variety of contexts and most of which are complex and non-routine. There is considerable responsibility and autonomy, and control or guidance of others is often required.

*Level 4*: competence in a broad range of complex, technical or professional work activities performed in a wide variety of contexts and with a substantial degree of personal responsibility and autonomy. Responsibility for the work of others and the allocation of resources is often present.

*Level 5*: competence which involves the application of a significant range of fundamental principles and complex techniques across a wide and often unpredictable variety of contexts. Very substantial personal autonomy and often significant responsibility for the work of others and for the allocation of substantial resources feature strongly, as do personal accountabilities for analysis and diagnosis, design, planning, execution and evaluation.

**Fig. 4.2:** The NVQ framework and levels
(*Source*: Hyland, 1994, p. 7)

Following a number of critical reviews and reports about the work of the NCVQ throughout the 1990s (Smithers, 1993; Marks, 1996; Beaumont, 1996; DfEE, 1997), the NCVQ was abolished in 1997 (though G/NVQs are still part of the system at the time of writing) and subsumed under the overarching Qualifications and Curriculum Authority (QCA). Hyland argued that NVQs – and indeed all programmes and qualifications supported by CBET functional analysis – were 'logically and conceptually confused, epistemologically ambiguous, and based on largely discredited behaviourist learning principles' (Hyland, 1994, p. x). This conclusion was supported by

| Higher Degree | (GNVQ5) | NVQ5 |
|---|---|---|
| Degrees | (GNVQ4) | NVQ4 |
| A/AS | Advanced GNVQ | NVQ3 |
| | Intermediate GNVQ | NVQ2 |
| GCSE | Foundation GNVQ | NVQ1 |

**Fig. 4.3:** The three-track qualifications framework
(*Source*: Hyland, 1999, p. 90)

philosophical argument, policy analysis and empirical research, and it would be useful to summarize the principal shortcomings of NVQs and the CBET approach which underpins them under the following headings.

### Inherent flaws and weaknesses

The replacement of traditional VET programmes with NVQs has led to widespread deskilling of occupational roles, a loss of significant theoretical content and a systematic narrowing and delimiting of vocational focus in fields such as construction (Callender, 1992), plumbing and electrical installation (Smithers, 1993), and in hairdressing, catering and business studies (Hyland and Weller, 1994). Perhaps this was to be expected from a system which, according to its proponents, is concerned only with the assessment of competence in the workplace and has 'nothing whatsoever to do with training or learning programmes' (Fletcher, 1991, p. 26). Raggat's (1994) survey of a wide range of NVQs offered in FE colleges concluded that staff considered the approach to be far too 'minimalist' with a content which was 'too narrow, concerned only with the performance of simple tasks' (p. 66).

The major Beaumont (1996) review of NVQs – despite the fact that it was accused by one of its more critical members, Alan Smithers, of soft-pedalling in order to hide fundamental problems and shortcomings – still could not disguise the fact that 'there was a lack of clarity about who [NVQs] are aimed at or what they relate to' and that the 'existence of concerns about consistency is enough in itself to threaten the credibility of NVQs' (Beaumont, 1996, pp. 2, 36, 38). More importantly, the many problems and anomalies subsumed under the innocuous and superficial label of 'language' problems in Beaumont were, for the most part, not superficial but quite serious defects inherent in the CBET system of functional analysis and its behaviourist underpinnings. As Ashworth (1992) concluded, the NCVQ system was seeking to implement an approach based on learning outcomes which was 'normally inappropriate to the description of human action or to the facilitation of the training of human beings' (p. 16). On a more practical level, Grugulis (2002) has argued that NVQs are almost always less effective in transmitting and assessing technical skills and knowledge than the qualifications they replace, and Oates (2004) suggests that occupational knowledge and practice cannot be adequately described by a series of technical statements of competence.

## Employer and industry involvement

A number of surveys in the 1990s indicated that employers – who are supposed to be the key players in the NCVQ system which prides itself on employer-defined standards – are ignorant or indifferent about NVQs or, where they have experience of them, see many faults with CBET. A national survey by the Further Education Funding Council (FEFC) revealed a 'widespread lack of knowledge about NVQs, particularly in small firms, and an unwillingness on the part of many of them to become involved in workplace training and assessment' (FEFC, 1994, p. 22), and similar findings were reported in a study by the Institute of Employment (IES, 1995).

As Smithers (1996) commented, the 'more employers know about NVQs the less they like them' (p. 2). Key factors in the low take-up of NVQs were reported in a survey by the National Foundation for Educational Research (NFER) in which 'the time and cost involved' and 'their perceived lack of credibility or commercial advantage' (Nichols, 1998, p. 36) were highlighted. Similarly, in the Ernst and Young (1995) evaluation of Modern Apprenticeships it was noted that one of the problems of encouraging employers to join the scheme was the difficulty of having to 'convince them of the benefits of NVQs' (p. 11). More recent DfES research has indicated that, even among those employers who have been persuaded to use NVQs, there are still complaints about the bureaucratic nature of the system and its lack of fit with current business needs (DfES, 2002a, para. 85). There is a special difficulty also with small employers – accounting for 90% of all firms and around 35% of the total workforce – who overwhelmingly view the NVQ system as being irrelevant to their requirements (Matlay and Hyland, 1997). The most recent survey of employer perceptions of NVQs (Roe *et al.*, 2006) painted a 'fairly negative picture' since 'fewer than half (45%) of all employers in England have any useful understanding of NVQ' (p. 75). The researchers go on to observe:

> Nor has NVQ achieved its original objectives to supplant existing qualifications and to become the major system by which vocational skills are certificated in England ... It appears that not only has NVQ not, as intended, reduced the immense array of existing qualifications, but has added its own substantial complexity to that array ... When it came to employer evaluations of NVQ, some further evidence of employers' more frequent preferences for non-NVQ qualifications came through. More employers would prefer candidates for recruitment to have a non-NVQ vocational qualification or an academic qualification than an NVQ. (*ibid.*, p. 75)

How are we to understand such findings against the background of the original claim that NVQs were designed to be employer led at all stages? There is, in fact, little evidence to support the claims about the 'employer-led' nature of competence standards and criteria of assessment. The occupational standards tend to be devised by certain approved private consultancies (Stewart and Sambrook, 1995), and the so-called employer representatives on Industry Lead Bodies tend to be made up of training and personnel managers plus a 'wide sprinkling of consultants, some of whom have a long history of involvement in the Employment Dept and its quangos' (Field,

1995, p. 37). Moreover, comparisons between different occupational groups in Britain, France and Germany (Prais, 1995; Green, 1995) have shown that NVQs are too narrow in scope and too concerned with lower-level, task-based activities to raise the general level of workforce skills. The vast majority of NVQs have been awarded at level 2 (DfES, 2006a, p. 3) – the equivalent of 5 GCSE grades at A–C – and there is still a dearth of intermediate technician qualifications at level 3 and above in areas of skills shortage. Level 2 NVQs, although formally equivalent to 5 good GCSEs, are not so in terms of the knowledge and skill that they presuppose. The idea that they are is one that needs to be questioned. Once it is questioned, then the whole National Qualification Framework (see Chapter 5) starts to look shaky. Such spurious 'equivalences' are a major skeleton in the cupboard of the English and Welsh qualification systems.

The Beaumont Report (1996) revealed that 90% of firms surveyed would only give credence to NVQs awarded by other employers – rather than by colleges or private training providers – yet the most recent statistics show that 82% of awards are made through the FE and private training routes (DfES, 2006a, p. 4). Nevertheless, these qualifications have some limited credence among employers and employees and if they were to be discredited that would be a major embarrassment for the English and Welsh qualification systems, not to mention those of the countries to whom they have been (astonishingly, given their obvious shortcomings) exported.

## Problems of assessment

There never has been much evidence to demonstrate the superiority of CBET over other systems of assessment (Tuxworth, 1989; Wolf, 1995). What needs to be added to the difficulties experienced over the last 20 years with NVQs is the growing body of evidence which indicates the vulnerability of the system to abuse and impropriety (Bell, 1996). In a 1993 Employment Department (ED) report on NVQ implementation, a number of 'assessment difficulties' were noted including 'the cost, the amount of paperwork involved, practical difficulties of assessment in the workplace, and problems about the reliability of assessments' (ED, 1993, p. 35). Similar problems of consistency were noted in the Beaumont review and reflected increased emphasis placed on requirements for 'sufficiency of evidence' (Bates and Dutson, 1995) in workplace assessments. Difficulties in ensuring reliability is a particular problem for CBET systems since they are based unashamedly on criterion-referencing with a primary emphasis on content validity. Such strategies are characterized by ever-increasing demands for specification of content and prescriptive procedures. As Wolf (1995) observes, the more systems are based on extremely demanding and rigid requirements – as has happened with NVQs – the more likely it becomes that factors which are technically extraneous to assessment will in fact preclude effective and high-quality assessment from taking place (p. 125).

In the more recent survey of employers' use and perceptions of NVQs, the researchers concluded that the 'attempt to specify competence in terms of extensive lists of behaviours leads to confusion, ambiguity and unreliability' (Roe et al., 2006, p. 6). The cost of adopting such approaches – influenced by Jessup's (1991) call for NCVQ assessments to 'just forget reliability altogether and concentrate on validity' (p. 191) – has been high indeed, and paid for by the many assessment anomalies and the correspondingly poor regard in which the qualifications are held.

In addition to such technical problems, the combination of a post-school funding regime based predominantly on outputs linked to the award of qualifications with an NVQ system defined in terms of outcomes – described by Hodkinson (1997) as a 'lethal cocktail' (p. 7) – resulted in assessment abuses on a large scale. A University of Sussex (1996) survey of NVQ assessment practices reported that almost 40% of assessors admitting passing sub-standard students, and this has been accompanied by a number of cases involving the award of certificates to 'bogus' students (Hyland, 1999). The 1997 report of the Public Accounts Committee (Baty, 1997) noted that 'incorrect' payments from the DfEE to NVQ providers had totalled £8.6 million in 1995/96, a figure which the education human rights charity Article 26 described as merely the tip of the corruption iceberg (Bell, 1996). Although it has to be said that assessment and monitoring has been tightened up in recent years following a number of government reviews – and also that anomalies can occur with any type of examination system – the peculiar nature of exclusively outcomes-based criterion-referencing strategies makes them extremely vulnerable in this respect.

Not only have CBET and NVQs failed to remedy the perennial difficulties of English VET, the NCVQ experiment has, arguably, served to downgrade the status of vocational studies by giving certain kinds of vocational training (as YTS did in the 1970s) a very bad name. NVQs are, of course, still part of the UK VET system though the original aims of covering the whole of the workforce with competence-based occupational standards were abandoned with the demise of the NCVQ.

It was, perhaps, unrealistic anyway to expect that a system which was, after all, designed solely for workplace assessment would have anything more than a 'niche' place in the national system. NVQs cover no more than 10–20% of occupationally related qualifications (with only 12% of the workforce holding an NVQ and 16% of employers in England using NVQs; Roe *et al.*, 2006, pp. 13, 75) and most learners in post-complulsory education and training – around three-quarters of all learners in the sector (DfES, 2006a) – are doing GNVQ programmes of broad vocationalism which involve a greater degree of knowledge about the target occupation, but rather less direct preparation for workplace competence. In addition, almost a million vocational awards made in 2004/05 fell outside the National Qualification Framework (NQF) of G/NVQs and Vocational Certificates of Education (vocational GCSEs/A-levels), amounting to around half of all vocational qualifications (*ibid.*, p. 1).

The fact that the NVQ system persists – and, indeed, has been exported to other countries – can be explained by the aggressive marketing and commercialism of the international market for pre-packaged VET commodities (Hyland, 1998, 2006b) combined with powerful political pressures concerned with face-saving (given the massive public investment in NVQs) and the irresistible appeal of apparently quick and easy solutions to difficult educational and economic problems. It was, for instance, obviously a rich mixture of largely noneducational and political vested interests which inspired the major project reported by Arguelles and Gonczi (2000) involving the mapping of the impact of CBET on educational systems in Mexico, Australia, New Zealand, Costa Rica, France and South Africa. The upshot of this massive public investment (with World Bank support) is summed up by Gonczi in the remarkably frank conclusion that:

> Industrial survival in the competitive workplace depends on innovative solutions to improvement which is the antithesis of prescribed procedures (as laid out in competency standards). We are left with the conclusion that the *foundation of the CBET system is shaky at best*. (*Ibid*., p. 26, emphasis added)

## Summary and conclusion

The obsession with narrow, mechanistic and unrealistic conceptions of skills and competences in recent VET reform programmes can be explained in terms of a mistaken reductionism motivated by the desire to find quick and easy solutions to long-standing and complex problems. However, both impoverished skill-talk and CBET are ill-founded, imprecise and anti-educational in their extremely limited conceptions of knowledge, theory and work-based learning. What is required to solve the perennial problems of VET is a genuinely national system of VET provision – involving the state partnerships of government, employers and unions characteristic of the French and German systems (Green, 1999) – VET programmes grounded in relevant knowledge, theory and values, and a qualifications framework in which vocational and academic tracks have parity of status and esteem in terms of overall planning and funding. Possibilities for the development of such a system are discussed in the final chapter, which examines recurrent themes in English VET against the background of recent policy trends. The next chapter looks in more detail at the peculiar nature and structure of VET provision in England.

# 5 'If You Can Understand It, You Deserve an NVQ Level 5': The Structure and Funding of Vocational Education in England

## Funding

Vocational education, as we have argued, is education whose overt purpose is to prepare people for participation in a sector of the labour market. Thus, although studying A-level Philosophy may ultimately assist you in your career, it is not offered or undertaken with that purpose in mind, while, for example, a National Diploma in Plumbing is. Vocational education takes place in schools, further education colleges, tertiary colleges, private training firms, workplaces and homes. Most of it is funded by the state, which uses monies raised from taxation for the purpose. There was a time when a form of hypothecated tax, the training levy, was used, but this has fallen into disuse. In what follows, we describe the main funding routes for vocational education in England.

## Department for Education and Skills (DfES)

School education is funded by the Department for Education and Skills, which devolves it to local education authorities (LEAs) which, in turn devolve the vast majority to individual school-administered budgets. A considerable amount of vocational education takes place within schools, both at the compulsory (Key Stage 4 – KS4) stage, and post-compulsory in sixth forms. In addition, some pupils at KS4 have the option to attend Further Education Colleges for up to two days a week to pursue vocational education, although this is financed by the colleges themselves and currently constitutes a form of cross-subsidization of school programmes. A variety of vocational qualifications exist for school education, including vocational GCSEs and GNVQs at levels 2 and 3. Many specialist schools offer programmes of vocational relevance in technology, business and sport, media and languages, without explicitly preparing young people for particular jobs. The aim, particularly at KS4, rather, is to allow young people to discover their own interests and abilities, to learn about the economic sector in which they are interested and to develop some generic skills relating to that sector. Such education can be called 'pre-vocational', as it gives young people the opportunity to learn about work, rather than preparing them explicitly to take part in it.

However, some programmes can properly be called 'weakly' rather than 'strongly' vocational (Stanton, 2004), even when they are not pre-vocational. Such programmes, including many level 3 GNVQ programmes, are taught in schools which do not have teaching staff with relevant industrial experience or purpose-built equipment and buildings. They do not give young people following their programmes the opportunity to practise the occupation in operational conditions. Neither do they give young people the opportunity to directly enter the labour market as qualified practitioners.

## The Learning and Skills Council

Funding for vocational education which is not part of higher education is provided via a national body called the Learning and Skills Council (LSC, 2001b). This funding is devolved via 47 regional Learning and Skills Councils which have responsibility for the funding and provision of education and training in FE and sixth-form colleges, work-based training for young people (including Modern Apprenticeships and Welfare to Work programmes), workforce development, adult and community learning, education/business links and advice and guidance for adult learners and employers through *Learndirect* and *Connexions* centres. The 'key tasks' of the LSC, outlined in its corporate plan (*ibid.*, p. 4), were listed as follows:

- To raise participation and achievement by young people
- To increase demand for learning by adults, and to equalize opportunities through better access to learning
- To engage employers in improving skills for employability and national competitiveness
- To raise the quality of education and training delivery
- To improve effectiveness and efficiency.

Although 'good progress' is said to have been made in all these areas in recent LSC reports announcing an increase in its budget for 2006/07 to £10.4 billion (LSC, 2005b), the shortfalls are also mentioned and can be clearly discerned in the government priorities cited in the publication of the 14–19 Skills Strategy (DfES, 2005b) and the recent FE White Paper (DfES, 2006b).


# Further Education (FE) Colleges

The bulk of non-school 16–19 education that is not school based is located in the further education colleges which are funded by the LSC. The origins of the colleges can be traced back to the Technical and Mechanics Institutes of the nineteenth century (Hyland and Merrill, 2003) but – since what was officially the first mention of the term in the 1944 Education Act (Dent, 1968) – FE institutions have become multifunctional agencies catering for an increasingly diverse student population. As Green and Lucas (1999) put it:

> Colleges appear to be meant to cater for everyone, 16–19 year olds, both academic and vocational, adult returners, access students, HE students, those with special needs, the socially excluded and those not involved anywhere else. As part of the growing ethic of lifelong learning, if you are not involved in a school sixth form, at work or at university, then you should be involved with the local college. (p. 35)

Moreover, each college has been shaped and defined to some extent by the influence of its own local education authority and the local economy and community surrounding it. As Ainley and Bailey (1997) point out, 'there is no such thing as a typical college' (p. 9). However, following the Foster Review of FE which recommended a 'core focus on skills and employability' (DfES, 2005c, p. 2), the most recent government line for the sector sees the central mission of colleges as 'delivering the skills and qualifications which individuals, employers and the economy need' (DfES, 2006a, p. 5).

There is nothing new about this mission, of course, since the sector was originally seen as the handmaiden of industry with its 'roots in the provision of technical and craft education for working-class men' (Leathwood, 1998, p. 256). What is new, however, is the diversity and range of VET offered in the colleges. This provision differs significantly from what is offered in most school settings in being more strongly vocational. Colleges usually specialize in one or more trade or industrial sector and tend to have purpose-built sites and specialist equipment, together with lecturers with considerable industrial experience in the relevant sector. Students typically study full time for level 2 or level 3 qualifications, either NVQs, Technical Certificates or Key Skills Certificates, or for qualifications that seek to unite theoretical and practical work within one qualification, such as the BTEC National Diplomas.

Strongly vocational work at levels 2 and 3 is not the only activity in such colleges. Many of them offer GCSEs, GNVQs and A-levels like the schools, either as an alternative for those who prefer a more adult environment or as a second chance for those who did not succeed very well in their school careers. In addition, the colleges provide a considerable amount of sub-NVQ work at entry level and, of increasing importance, both vocational and academic provision at level 4 and above, ranging from HNC to HND to Foundation Degree to Honours Degree work. This is funded by the Higher Education Funding Council for England (HEFCE). Some colleges have so much of this work that they are known as 'mixed economy colleges' (just over 10% of HE is now delivered in such institutions; HEFCE, 2004) and some of this group have aspirations to be incorporated into the higher education sector as university colleges, though the thrust of the recent Foster Review of FE was distinctly critical of such mission drift (DfES, 2005c).

One important feature of study in an FE college should be borne in mind. In most cases, those who attend are students of the college. They may be in a workplace for a part of their course, but they do not have the status of employees in the workplace. They will pursue the academic and work-related parts of their courses within the college. Thus although the programmes offered in an FE college are usually more strongly vocational than those offered in schools, it may be doubted whether, in every single case, they are strongly vocational enough to make the qualified student directly employable. There are a number of reasons why this might be so. First, the occupational skills learned on a course may not match the job- and task-specific skills required by an employer. Second, relevant work experience may be non-existent or limited; and finally because, although the student may have had ample opportunity to practise skills in the controlled simulatory environment of a college workshop, he or she will not have had sufficient opportunity to do so in workplace operational conditions, where safety factors, time criticality and mutual dependence of members of a team may be essential to successful work, or even to the avoidance of disaster. There is some evidence that there may be a mismatch between the skill set provided by the college and that required by the employer in some sectors, for example construction (see also Hayward, 2004).

## Private training providers

In addition to the largely publicly funded further education colleges, there are many private training providers who educate students on behalf of firms, often for a component of an apprenticeship scheme. Much of the money that flows to private training providers comes, ultimately, from the public purse as, for example, is the case with Modern Apprenticeships, from which a significant proportion of the finance comes from the LSC budget. These private training providers vary greatly in size and competence (Farlie, 2004).

# Apprenticeship

As we have already noted, apprenticeship is a very old and well-established form of strong vocational education with its roots in medieval Europe. With the exception of those countries that operate the Dual System, which is itself a very heavily modified form of apprenticeship, it now has a relatively minor role in vocational education in Britain (under 10% of the proportion of 16-year-olds in education and training in 2002). Nearly all apprenticeship in Britain now comes under the government-sponsored Apprenticeship (formerly Modern Apprenticeship) system, whereby employers receive a government subsidy for taking on apprentices as employees. Foundation Apprenticeships are meant to result in a level 2 qualification, Advanced Apprenticeships to result in a qualification at level 3 and Graduate Apprenticeships at level 4. Although the completion rates for apprenticeships have improved from 31% to 40% in the last few years, the overall take-up in this sphere is still far below that of Germany and France, and we rank 24th out of 29 developed nations in terms of overall post-16 VET participation (DfES, 2006a, pp. 2–3). All this must be a major cause for concern for educators and policy-makers since apprenticeship has some widely recognized advantages as a form of strongly vocational education. First, it equips young people directly for employment in the sector within which they work. Second, it provides an environment for growing up in, which many young people find attractive. Third, in its modern form, it can, through links with colleges, provide the underpinning knowledge necessary for work in a high-skill economic environment.

However, there are also a number of problems with maintaining apprenticeship as a significant sector of Britain's vocational education provision. Political imperatives have led to the misleading classification as 'apprenticeship' of schemes which are more akin to work experience programmes and which do not contain the skill formation that apprenticeship schemes are supposed to contain. This tends to discredit apprenticeship as a valuable mode of vocational education. This is connected to another problem, the wide perception, often among schoolteachers, that apprenticeship is a low-status and second-best alternative to more academic forms of education. Then there is a problem of widely differing quality of provision among different employers and training providers. Some apprenticeship schemes, especially those offered by 'blue chip' companies, are of a very high quality indeed and are much sought after. Others are of indifferent quality. Many sectors of the economy either do not have an apprenticeship tradition or, because of the skill configuration of the sector, have little need for apprentices. Others again, which do have skill needs, have evolved in such a way that they are no longer able to easily provide apprenticeships. For example, construction, which relies on subcontracting to small firms, no longer has much capacity to train the people that it needs. The large firms rely on subcontractors to actually carry out the work while these are too small to be able to afford to take on apprentices.

## The qualification structure of VET

The qualification structure of VET in England and Wales is quite difficult to understand, despite attempts over the years to make it more comprehensible. This is partly because it has not, historically, been centrally administered and partly because it has been, and continues to be, subjected to continual change. The first thing to be said about this system is that VET qualifications have now been classified within a broader *National Qualifications Framework*, of eight levels, from 1 to 8, with a further three entry levels below level 1. The intention is that vocational qualifications can be assigned an academic qualification equivalent, as shown in Figure 5.1.

Vocational qualifications can be classified into various families within this overarching framework. One group, exemplified by the GNVQ, is holistic in the sense that it integrates practical and theoretical elements, but is also weakly vocational in the sense described above. These qualifications are available at levels 1 and 2 of the NQF. The next group is a holistic, more strongly vocational qualification called the National Diploma. This is available at levels 2, 3 and 4. There is also a part-time variant of the level 4 qualification. These are

| National Qualifications Framework (NQF) | | Framework for Higher Education Qualifications (FHEQ) |
|---|---|---|
| **Previous levels (Examples)** | **Current levels (Examples)** | **Levels (Examples)** |
| **Level 5** Level 5 NVQ in Construction | **Level 8** Specialist awards | **D (doctoral)** Doctorates |
| Level 5 Diploma in Translation | **Level 7** Level 7 Diploma in Translation | **M (masters)** Masters degrees, postgraduate certificates and diplomas |
| **Level 4** Level 4 National Diploma in Professional Production Skills | **Level 6** Level 6 National Diploma in Professional Production Skills | **H (honours)** Bachelor degrees, graduate certificates and diplomas |
| Level 4 BTEC Higher National Diploma in 3D Design  Level 4 Certificate in Early Years Practice | **Level 5** Level 5 BTEC Higher National Diploma in 3D Design | **I (intermediate)** Diplomas of higher education and further education, foundation degrees and higher national diplomas |
| | **Level 4** Level 4 Certificate in Early Years Practice | **C (certificate)** Certificates of higher education |
| **Level 3** Level 3 Certificate in Small Animal Care Level 3 NVQ in Aeronautical Engineering A-levels | | |
| **Level 2** Level 2 Diploma for Beauty Specialists Level 2 NVQ in Agricultural Crop Production GCSEs Grades A★–C | | |
| **Level 1** Level 1 Certificate in Motor Vehicle Studies Level 1 NVQ in Bakery GCSEs Grades D–G | | |
| **Entry level** Entry Level Certificate in Adult Literacy | | |

**Fig. 5.1:** The current Qualifications Framework

rarely offered in schools but much more frequently offered in FE colleges which have the equipment and staff to cope with their more strongly vocational requirements.

The currently best-known type of vocational qualification in the field is the NVQ which was discussed at length in the previous chapter. Although offered at five levels, 60% or so of awards are made at the levels 1–3 with the vast majority made at level 2. In addition, almost a million vocational awards made in 2004/05 fell outside the National Framework, amounting to around half of all vocational qualifications (DfES, 2006a, pp. 1–2). The NVQ is, both in historical and international terms, an unusual kind of qualification and deserves further scrutiny. It is relatively recent, having first been introduced by the NCVQ in 1986 and is explicitly described as a competence-based qualification. As we have seen in the previous two chapters, the term 'competence' is quite a slippery and often, in the way that it is used, misleading concept. The notion of 'competence' which is intended, however, is one that is based on job- or task-specific importance. To quote Gilbert Jessup, one of the architects of these qualifications, 'Skills can only be demonstrated through their application in performance (doing something) while knowledge can be elicited through the more abstract means of conversation, questioning or working' (1991, p. 121). In other words, the emphasis is on the directly observable, practical ability rather than on underpinning knowledge. This approach to vocationally relevant knowledge has already been discussed and criticized in the previous chapter.

A distinctive feature of the NVQ is that it accredits current ability to perform a range of tasks. It is not attached to a curriculum framework, although there is no reason why someone should not follow a programme of training in order to obtain an NVQ. It is, however, perfectly possible to obtain one through the *accreditation of prior experiential learning* (APEL), rather than through study. It certifies that one has certain skills, not that one has been through a course of study or training.

The disconnection of NVQ, especially at levels 1–3, from underpinning knowledge, has caused dissatisfaction in some sectors where it is thought that underpinning knowledge is actually important for effective performance. On the other hand, it is also true that some major employers have discarded the NVQ approach because they find the accreditation process too bureaucratic (Hyland, 1999) and place more emphasis on the so-called 'soft skills' which are really personal attributes, for example in the financial sector. Because of the concern about under-pinning knowledge, *technical certificates*, which provide the cor-relative underpinning knowledge related to NVQs at levels 2 and 3, were introduced some years ago. Although technical certificates are related to NVQs they are taught and examined separately. A problem that arises is that of *integration*, namely whether, if underpinning knowledge is necessary for perfor-mance, it can be successfully deployed when taught and exam-ined separately from the skills that it is supposed to underpin. If the point of the possession of underpinning knowledge is that it can be used to inform practical judgements in workplace situa-tions, then there is a danger that, by refraining from teaching it in such a way that one learns to use it in practical workplace situations, one is in fact failing to ensure that it is integrated into workplace judgement. In fact, there is some evidence that this is recognized as a problem, as seen in the report by the QCA (2004b) on the relationship between technical certificates and NVQs. At its worst, the technical certificate could be seen as a bolt-on extra to the NVQ once the inadequacies of the latter had been recognized. Some sectors are currently trying to dis-pense with the technical certificate and attempt to teach and certify underpinning knowledge in other ways.

It has also been recognized that the NVQ has shortcomings in another dimension as well. One of the complaints of employers over the years has been the lack of knowledge on the part of employees of so-called 'key skills' of numeracy, com-munication, self-management of performance, information and communication technology and problem-solving. Although these 'skills' are not task or even sector specific it is arguable that they are necessary for many jobs, although perhaps not for very low-skilled ones, of which there are many in the British economy (see Chapter 6). They are also promoted by the government as an essential component of Apprenticeship qualifications, which, typically although not universally, require a minimum of NVQ, Technical Certificate and Key Skills certification (sometimes these are not considered to be sufficient – see Gospel and Fuller, 1998). They are considered to be important because of the *flexibility* that they help bestow on workers moving from job to job, but also because of the significance that they have as a marker of a basic general education and as a necessary component of citizenship, where being able to understand social, economic and political processes is a basic requirement. However, they have encountered considerable resistance on the part of both apprentices and students and on the part of employers. One of the problems with Key Skills mirrors that encountered with the technical certificates, namely the detachment of the KS component of an Apprenticeship qualification from the technical knowledge and practical abilities requirements.

On the other hand, it is also true to say that the NVQ, at least in certain sectors, has established itself and gained approval from employers and young people alike. For some employers, the ability to provide *in situ* certification of skill with only the amount of training required for the job specification fits attractively with their own perceived skill needs, which are often very undemanding. Employees, whose experience of academic work has been mixed, and who wish to avoid further study in favour of practical activity, also find the NVQ a congenial qualification (QCA, 2004b). The more general point about the status and future of NVQs is that they will live and die by the perceived appropriateness to different employers in different sectors of the economy. In some cases, as with some sections of banking, they will not be perceived to be appropriate, because of the prior importance attached to personality and deportment and to externally unsupported in-house training (Hoare, 2006). On the other hand, in other sectors such as engineering, they may be thought to be an insufficient guarantee that an apprentice is fully qualified and may be supplemented with an appropriate national diploma (Gospel and Fuller, 1998). The more general point here is that the British qualification system is employer driven and the perceived needs of employers in different sectors of the economy differ greatly. One cannot, therefore, expect to find much in the way of national patterns in such a system.

The NVQ is a relatively new development in the area of vocational qualifications and much hope was pinned on it as a global, unifying model for vocational qualifications across nearly all sectors. However, the shortcomings of this approach to the certification of practical knowledge are becoming increasingly apparent and, as a result, the virtues of more traditional qualifications are, once again, receiving attention. The problem has already been stated briefly but it is worth re-emphasizing to bring out what the difference between the more traditional type of vocational qualification and the NVQ really is. When the ability required to do a job is the routine performance of a very limited range of tasks which require neither underpinning knowledge nor the need for complex judgement, as it often is in the British economy, then the abilities required for an NVQ may be sufficient to do the job, although in the absence of a key skill such as literacy this may be difficult for some jobs. With anything more complex, however, such observable behaviours cannot adequately describe the abilities needed. As explained in the previous chapter, one of the difficulties is that a simplistic notion of observable behaviour may, in this context, be a misleading account of the kinds of *actions* required in more complex tasks, where planning, judgement and evaluation are key parts of the action.

Such frameworks raise a number of questions, but the main one concerns whether the proclaimed equivalence of qualifications really is a meaningful equivalence. The National Qualifications Framework suggests that this is so, but there is a really serious difficulty in establishing this. The idea of equivalence in a qualification framework is that the level of achievement in one type of qualification is at least roughly the same as that of another qualification at the same level. But when one is comparing an essentially practical qualification with an academic one, one is in danger of making comparisons between achievements that are not relevantly like each other. The problem is not so acute with the technical certificates and the key skills, since they certify knowledge that fits into an academic framework, either propositional knowledge or academically related skills such as literacy or numeracy. The problem is also, arguably, a manageable one when one is comparing an integrated qualification such as a National Diploma or a GNVQ with a GCSE or an AS-level. We can allow that presumed equivalence may not reflect the actual level of achievement in the two qualifications, so that, for example, the intermediate GNVQ may not be regarded by external audiences as having the currency that the NQF says that it has. But such difficulties are, in principle, resolvable by negotiation. The idea here is that there is a trade-off between, on the one hand, achievement of academic knowledge and, on the other hand, the achievement of integrated underpinning knowledge with practical ability. We could say that although the underpinning knowledge in the vocational qualification is not as extensive or, maybe, as rigorous as it is with the academic qualification, nevertheless the achievement of an integrated practical ability is a sufficiently demanding achievement for a credible equivalence to be claimed.

However, this move will not really work with levels 1–3 of the NVQ, where the underpinning knowledge required is minimal and is often regarded by employers as dispensable. On what basis can we justifiably claim the equivalence of, for example, an NVQ 2 in Scaffolding with a C pass in GCSE Maths, when the abilities required in each are so different and, in the case of the NVQ, require no significant underpinning knowledge? One may then, in the absence of a move towards integrated vocational qualifications, be sceptical about such integrated qualification frameworks. However, they have real currency and, as part of the European Union Lisbon process of integrating the European labour market, will form a constituent of a European-wide comparator of vocational qualifications, which are themselves of widely different kinds.

## Permeability and progression

The level at which a qualification is positioned is not just a matter of 'academic' interest, it is also of considerable practical consequence for the individual aspiring to possess or possessing the qualification. The question of whether qualifications are meaningfully comparable is highly relevant to this point. Some qualifications are 'permeable' and are designed to be so. Two or more qualifications are permeable if the one that is at a lower level serves as a sufficient entry point for moving to the qualification at a higher level. The idea of permeability is thus linked to that of a level. For example, a GCSE is a staging post on the way to an A/AS-level qualification if someone wishes to pursue his or her studies and the A/AS is itself, in turn, a staging post on the way to a Bachelors degree. Setting up an integrated qualification framework gives a *formal* equivalence and a *theoretical* possibility of moving from one level to another provided one's initial qualification is at the right level. England has adopted principles within a credit framework which set out the formal possibilities of progression through a permeable qualification framework (QCA, 2004b).

However, what is theoretically possible through a formal equivalence may well not be *practically* possible, because *informally* the lower-level qualification may *not* be regarded as a sufficient criterion for initiating the process of movement to a qualification at the next level. In such situations, qualifications routes that appear to be permeable are, in fact, not so or are so to a very limited extent. This is an issue that ramifies through the British vocational qualification system. Thus, for example, we know that take-up of level 3 NVQs by holders of level 2 NVQs in the same sector is very low. We also know that, for example, some employers and admissions tutors are reluctant to regard an advanced GNVQ as equivalent to two A-levels. The first point relates to the fact that even the relatively modest underpinning knowledge required by NVQ 3 may be beyond the scope of someone capable of achieving an NVQ level 2. A related problem here may well be that someone capable of achieving an NVQ level 2 in Scaffolding would not be capable of achieving a GCSE C grade in an academic subject. If this is so, then it casts some doubt on the claimed equivalence of level 2 qualifications and on the claimed permeability of the structure.

A further source of confusion is that, in higher education, a different system of qualification levels has been in operation, although it has now been integrated into the National Qualifications Framework (see above). According to the Quality Assurance Agency (QAA, 2001) the following five levels apply to all HE awards in England, Wales and Northern Ireland:

1  Certificates of Higher Education (NQF 4).
2  Foundation Degrees, ordinary (Bachelors) degrees, Diplomas of Higher Education (NQF 5).
3  Bachelors degrees with Honours, Graduate Certificates and Graduate Diplomas (NQF 6).
4  Masters Degrees, Postgraduate Certificates and Postgraduate Diplomas (NQF 7).
5  Doctorates (NQF 8).

(Based on QAA, 2001, p. 3)

Moreover, the level descriptors for the intermediate level of Foundation and Ordinary Degrees indicate that these qualifications signify that the holders of such qualifications will 'have developed a sound understanding of the principles in their field of study' which will 'have had a vocational orientation, enabling them to perform effectively in their chosen field'. At level 3, however, an Honours graduate 'will have developed an understanding of a complex body of knowledge, some of it at the current boundaries of an academic discipline' (ibid., p. 1). Not only do such hard and fast distinctions appear to be epistemologically questionable since it is difficult to pin down qualification specifications with such exactness, but also the whole national qualifications system – involving a mix of the NCVQ-based levels from GCSE to Doctoral level and the QAA system covering only HE levels – is utterly confused as it inherits the problems both of the old NCVQ system and those of the HEFCE, and thus makes attempts to determine equivalence or comparative status look misleadingly simple. Certainly, any claims about permeability would be difficult to test within the framework of the current system.

Finally, there are cases of relative permeability where two or more qualifications at the same level in the qualification framework may not share the same degree of permeability. For example, of two level 5 qualifications, the Higher National Diploma and the Foundation Degree, it is normally the case that, in the former case, progression to a level 6 qualification, such as a Bachelor's degree may take six months or a year more study than for the holder of a Foundation Degree.

The permeability issue is of profound importance for at least two reasons. First, because permeability opens up ways of increasing skill levels without wasteful and demoralizing time spent on unnecessary study. One should not need to study or practise the same material twice or study more than is necessary in order to progress to the next level. Second, permeability is also a potential instrument for social inclusion, whereby individuals with low-level vocational qualifications can progress to higher academic qualifications in their sector as part of their career progress but also as a way of ensuring social mobility. As things currently stand, the British qualification system is a long way from ensuring qualification permeability. Furthermore, as suggested, the rather sharp break in academic content between some vocational qualifications and academic qualifications that are nominally at the same level casts doubt on the current level classification which underpins the formal notion of permeability.

## Participation in VET and trends

England and the UK generally stand out from the countries in Northwestern Europe in terms of the relatively low rate of participation in education after the age of 16. This contrasts with the high rate of participation in higher education of around 42%. Thus in 2001, 74.7% of 15- to 19-year-olds in the UK were enrolled in some form of education. This contrasts with France at 86.6%, Germany at 89.4% and the Netherlands at 87.2%. These figures by themselves, however, conceal other trends, as Figure 5.2 demonstrates.

We need to distinguish between general vocational tracks which do not directly prepare young people to become employees, such as GNVQs and, to some extent, National Diplomas and Certificates, from those which are directly related to the workplace (see Figure 5.3). When the numbers are broken down in this way, it can be seen that the lack of significant decline in 16–19 participation as a whole is due to the increase in numbers staying on in full-time education, whether in school, sixth form or tertiary college or in a further education

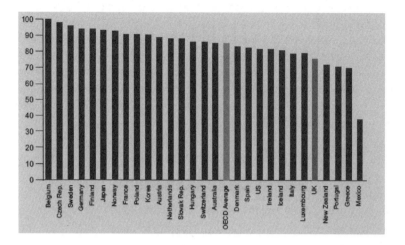

**Fig. 5.2:** International comparisons of participation in education and training at 17 in 2002
(*Source*: DfES, 2005)

college. The numbers participating in government- and employer-funded training appears to be in decline.

The FTE component of these numbers consists of students studying A-levels to go on to university and those following a number of level 2 and level 3 vocationally related programmes such as National Diplomas and GNVQs. Those funded by government and employers will include people on Foundation (level 2) and Advanced (level 3) Modern Apprenticeships. The significance of the FTE figures is that the vocational component in them may be exaggerated. This is because a significant number of these qualifications are what Stanton (2004) calls 'weakly' as opposed to 'strongly' vocational (see above). Since these qualifications do not directly fit their holders for participation in the labour market they are undertaken for a variety of reasons, one of which may well be to provide an alternative form of liberal education to the A-level.

Higher education for these purposes is a programme that leads to a qualification at NQF level 4 or above. Further education consists of all work for the 16+ age group from non-awarding bearing courses to entry level 1 and up to NQF level 3. The figures set out in Figure 5.4 suggest that participation in

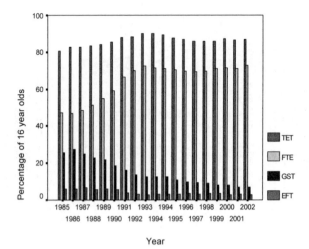

**Fig. 5.3:** The percentage of 16-year-olds participating in different modes of education and training (TET = Total Education and Training; FTE = Full-time education; GST = Government-supported training; EFT = Employer-funded training)
(*Source*: DfES, 2002b, 2004b)

non-HE study has started to decline gently among the 16–19 age group.

Not only, therefore, is there an overall decline in numbers following a vocational route, but the more strongly vocational routes, principally funded by government and employers, which is already relatively insignificant, is in serious decline. Such a situation hardly bodes well for a government keen to increase the availability of skills in economic demand. However, developments underway at the time of writing are designed to address some of these issues.

## What of the future?

The UK government is, thus, aware of these problems and is seeking to address them through legislation, by unifying 18–19 exit qualifications in an overarching diploma at levels 1–3. As a preliminary, they published a White Paper on 14–19 Education and have emphasized two significant issues. The first is that the diploma will be a kind of envelope for existing qualifications

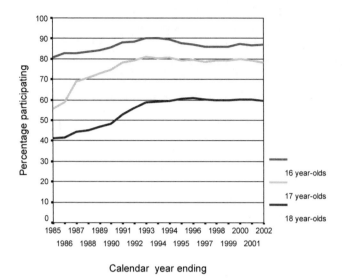

**Fig. 5.4** Total participation in education and training by 16- to 18-year-olds in England: 1985–2002
(*Source*: Hayward, 2004)

such as A-levels, although some qualifications, such as the GNVQ, will no longer exist. Instead, employers will have a significant role (assuming they take it up) in constructing new vocational qualifications which will fit into the overarching diploma structure. The government seems to be aware of the problem of 'weak' vocational qualifications and hopes to address it with employer-designed qualifications that involve real work experience and industrially experienced teachers. To the same end the overall vocational mission of post-school education and training will – as the recent White Paper responds to the Foster review of the sector – be re-aligned to meet the 'two strategic challenges of transforming 14–19 education and up-skilling the adult workforce' (DfES, 2006b, p. 3). Students will be able to combine strongly vocational with academic qualifications in different ways in order to obtain the diploma, so it is envisaged that those who do not wish to let go of some element of liberal education in their 18+ qualification will be able to do so, as well as gaining a worthwhile vocational qualification. It will be interesting to see if employers rise to the challenge that the government has set them by designing such qualifications and helping to provide the teachers, equipment and buildings that such courses need. There may be some difficulty with this, however, for reasons that will become plainer when we look at the demand for skills and how this affects the youth labour market in the next chapter.

# 6 You Take the High Skills Road and I'll Take the Low Skills Road

## The problem identified in Chapter 2: the role of employers

It has become customary in recent years to classify some economies as 'high skill' and others as 'low skill' (see, for example, Ashton and Green, 1996). This is not a judgement about their success but about the degree to which they depend on skilled labour. An economy can be successfully run on a low-skill basis provided that it maintains good growth and low unemployment, even though productivity per man hour may not be all that impressive. Britain is often thought to be a low-skill economy, France and Germany high-skill economies and the United States a mixed variant. Britain, as many people are fond of telling us, is a highly successful economy, with the virtue of 'flexibility', by which its advocates mean loose employment laws and a low level of regulation. The kind of skill mix that an economy requires has profound importance for vocational education. It is very important when high levels of skill are required, much less so when they are not. The evidence is that British employers make relatively few skill demands on their employees and, consequently, have relatively little demand for skills and hence for vocational education. This may come as a bit of a surprise for those who, listening to the rhetoric about the 'knowledge economy', the 'skills revolution' and the importance of education for the economy, may have been led to believe that we are in the midst of an economic transformation which involves a highly educated, highly skilled workforce. But it is, nevertheless, true, as this chapter will seek to establish.

## The supply of skills and the demand for them

Following the work of David Finegold (1991), one can classify the relationship between a successful economy and its skill level as an 'equilibrium' or arrangement that yields a satisfactory outcome to the interested parties. Thus, in a 'high-skill equilibrium', highly skilled, highly paid employees produce high-cost, high-specification, high-quality goods and services which can not only be exported but, perhaps, more importantly, can be afforded in the domestic market by highly paid workers and their families. The high skills are a crucial ingredient in the production of high-specification, high-quality goods. By contrast, a 'low-skill equilibrium' relies on the production of low-cost, low-specification and (possibly) low-quality goods and services which can be afforded by those on a low budget, either overseas or domestically. This is a model of 'ideal types'. It is possible for different sectors of a national economy to operate at different equilibrium levels and it is possible for national economies to position themselves at different points on a continuum of skill mix (Iversen, 2005). Nevertheless, one can usefully distinguish between different economies in this way.

We have already noted in Chapter 4 how elastic the use of the term 'skill' has become. This is particularly the case in the debate concerning the role of skills and knowledge in developing the economy. Bearing in mind our strong reservations about the promiscuous use of the term 'skill', we will, nevertheless, use it as a shorthand term in this chapter to refer to all the knowledge and abilities that employees and employers bring to bear on their work. They will also have knowledge and ability, often gained in formal education, that is not used at work. However, we also need to bear in mind that something that one has learned for one purpose (e.g. gardening for leisure) may, in appropriate circumstances, be used at work, for example, when through redundancy an amateur gardener takes up new employment in a garden centre.

## Skills and qualifications distinguished

Depending on the level of 'skill' an economy requires to operate efficiently, there will, according to economic theory, be a corresponding demand for those skills in the labour market. The labour market will send signals to prospective employees about the kind and level of skill required and individuals will respond to these signals by acquiring skills in demand by employers. In the ultra-rational, calculative world beloved of some economists, individuals will make decisions about investment in their own skills, based on a perception of the (discounted) returns available to them in exchange for direct financial outlay and the opportunity cost incurred in undertaking training. If the lifetime employment returns are positive, then individuals will train; if not, they will not (Ashton and Green, 1996, ch. 2). Serious doubts can be raised about the realism of this picture, known as 'Human Capital Theory', but let us accept it at face value for the moment.

It follows that decisions to undertake post-compulsory education will be largely based on economic calculation and that training will only be undertaken if it provides a return. A complicating factor is that educational qualifications, particularly those that do not have a direct vocational benefit, may be undertaken for other reasons, such as the love of a subject or for social prestige. It further follows that negative labour market signals will dampen the demand for education and training, as they will indicate poor returns available. On the other hand, it may be the case that people will undertake education for non-vocational reasons, or for only partly vocational reasons, two of which have already been mentioned. Other reasons may include *positional advantage* and *gains accruing from increased productivity*. The positional advantage to be gained from education arises from the fact that although one's educational qualification may not be of direct economic value, it is an indirect indicator of the desirability of an employee. First, a good qualification is a 'filter' distinguishing a candidate from others and, second, it may be an indication of intelligence or persistence and thus of character attributes that may be of potential value to an employer (a secondary indicator of 'skill' in this broad sense).

It follows from these considerations that we should carefully distinguish between: (a) the skills needed to carry out a job and the qualifications that indicate that one has such skills; (b) the currency of job-related skills and education-based qualifications; (c) skills specific to a job and skills that an educational qualification signifies which could be useful in a job. It is usual for discussions of the relationship between skills and the economy not to distinguish sufficiently between these (e.g. Warhurst *et al.*, 2004). Let us look first at the distinction between skills and qualifications. From a narrow employer perspective the important thing is for an employee to be able to do the job assigned. The employer is not particularly keen on a qualification that may make the employee more mobile, liable to employment by rival firms. Skill qualifications may, therefore, underestimate the real amount of skill available in a section of the workforce. But much of this skill may be highly firm specific and not easily transferable. Here is an area of skill formation that vocational educators may not easily gain access to. To take the second distinction, it is a mistake to assume that an economy based on high skills is necessarily signified by high levels of education; it may be the case that the education in question is not of immediate relevance to economic efficiency. Formal levels of educational achievement should not necessarily be taken as indicators of level of skill. Third, it may nevertheless be the case that there is an economic benefit to be had from an employer in the 'transferable skills' that the holder of an education qualification may possess. These skills may, however, still be less useful than skills developed especially for a job or an occupation.

## What the theory of markets should tell us about skill supply

What do these considerations tell us about the demand for education and skills in the UK? On the one hand, economic considerations seem to suggest that where there is a low employer demand for skills, this will translate into a low employee demand for the acquisition of such skills. Thus, a 'low-skill equilibrium' will entail a low demand for skills acquisition from labour market entrants. This suggests a demand-led model of skill acquisition. However, classical economics suggests a different picture. 'Say's law' suggests that the supply of a commodity will always achieve a demand for it (Pen, 1970). The important proviso, of course, is that the price for the commodity must be right. This supply-based model suggests that one should develop the skills and wait for demand to pick up. However, this approach is in potential conflict with the human capital model of motivation described earlier. According to the supply-based model, there will be a clearing price for labour; according to the human capital model, the price of an individual's labour has to match the outlay required to gain the necessary skills. Too much supply of a given kind of labour will eventually disrupt the employee demand for skills, since their acquisition will not be appropriately remunerated.

Neither the human capital model nor the supply-based model can be assumed to work as economic models suggest they should, so we should, perhaps, treat them with some caution. In practice, there are skill surpluses and skill shortages and a lag between supply and demand which often leads to unemployment and insecurity among those who have spent a great deal on acquiring their skills. When the labour market is insecure and/or unpredictable, and the welfare costs of investing in the wrong skills are high, it is easy for potential employees to adopt a conservative strategy and to spend little on skill acquisition and to rely on a low-skill labour market (Iversen, 2005). Employers, too, face problems. When the demand for certain skills is high and the supply tight, they face risks moving from low-cost, low-specification markets to high-cost, high-specification ones. A conservative product strategy makes sense, particularly if one's domestic market is only able to pay a limited price for goods and services. There are other risks, associated with employer-funded training, which must be taken into account. An employer who trains an apprentice or worker at his own expense makes an investment that cannot be recouped if his rivals use the savings that they make by not training to 'poach' the employee who has been trained. The rational strategy in this situation is not to train. This is a classic example of a 'Prisoner's Dilemma' co-ordination problem, where it is rational for the parties involved to adopt sub-optimal solutions because there is no way of co-ordinating activities to bring about better solutions.

This type of scenario tends to occur in de-regulated economies and labour markets where welfare provision is poor or mediocre, as in contemporary Britain. There are solutions to problems of skill demand and supply, economic adaptation and low educational aspirations, but they depend on government action which interferes with the freedom of employers to run the labour market in a way that they feel suits them. The key problem for a country, if it wishes to 'upskill' its labour force, is to create a demand for high skills among employers in the first instance. This is likely to create a demand from potential employees, if other conditions are right. As we saw, this does not necessarily mean creating a demand for high levels of non-vocational education, if these have a very limited effect on economic success. Having a degree may increase one's positional advantage in a general labour market and may even increase one's productivity, but if it is not in a subject which contains skill and knowledge in demand on the labour market, the presence of large numbers of people with such qualifications is only going to have a limited effect on 'upskilling'. If one were to look at the matter cynically, one could suggest that a government that wanted to be seen to be 'upskilling' the labour force without interfering with the prerogatives of employers, would adopt just such a strategy and would seek to recoup costs by adopting a human capital model based on loans and repayable tuition fees.

One common refrain of the government is that the enhancement of skills is the key to productivity and that our national performance in terms of productivity per man hour is low, particularly at the technician grade where skills that imply a level 3 qualification are normally required (HM Treasury, 2000; DfES, 2005b). Employers must want workers with level 3 skills in order for them to be employed and the lack of employer demand suggests that they may not be necessary to their business strategy, despite the poor productivity record of the British worker. While poor productivity may make it difficult for firms to compete in some markets, there is enough domestic demand for the products and services of British firms for this not to be a significant worry. Indeed, figures published by the government (DfES, 2003, p. 39) suggest that, over the next six years, demand for skills at levels 1, 2 and 3 is likely to remain flat, while there will be some demand for an increase in level 4 and above qualifications. This does not suggest the existence of strong incentives for study at these levels, and poor returns on level 2 qualifications suggest, from a human capital point of view, that these are of limited value. It is not entirely surprising, then, that so many young people are turning to higher education to boost their educational qualifications and their employability. Whatever the doubts about whether or not level 4+ education is a good investment in human capital terms, it looks like a better bet, in general terms, than qualification at level 3 and especially below level 3.

These considerations suggest that the demand of employers for skills is the crucial factor in determining whether or not young people choose to invest in vocational qualifications. One does not have to be a naïve believer in Human Capital Theory to see this. Although young people may have a far from perfect knowledge of what the labour market will require when they qualify, they have a good sense that the returns on some qualifications are low and that there may be various advantages to study at higher education level. The evidence suggests that employer demand for vocational qualifications at level 3 and below is quite limited, while levels 4+, whether vocational or non-vocational, may confer some advantages in the labour market. None of this should really be surprising. The surprising thing, in a way, is the continuance of rhetoric about the need for skills and the demands of the 'knowledge economy' when the evidence, in the UK at least, seems to point in the other direction. Neither should we be particularly surprised that the UK continues to operate as a 'low-skill equilibrium'; there are not sufficient incentives for employers to invest in skills and the government is clearly unwilling to employ measures that would oblige them to do so.

## Is a low-skill equilibrium desirable?

One may ask 'Why does this matter?' After all, Britain has a prosperous economy with low unemployment and one could say that we all benefit from this arrangement. Young people have ready access to the labour market, which most of their compatriots in Northern Europe do not; consumers benefit from cheap labour in the service sector; and, as already remarked, unemployment is relatively low. The consequences of running our economy in this way are profound. Perhaps the most important point concerns education. Just under 50% of 16-year-olds fail to reach the official 'employability' level of 5 A*–C grades at GCSE; participation in work-based learning is in decline and 16+ participation rates are among the lowest in Europe. Notoriously in the UK vocational education does not suffer from a lack of 'parity of esteem' with academic qualification, it suffers from a lack of esteem. Our low educational achievement and the projected continuing lack of demand for skills, despite years of reform to both the school and the vocational education systems, suggest that we are a long way from participating in the much-hyped 'knowledge economy' and that 'lifelong learning' remains largely a fantasy of policy-makers. In addition, one could maintain that the abilities of much of the population are not used and that millions are condemned to low-paid and uninteresting jobs. Questions may also be raised concerning whether such a state of affairs is sustainable in the longer term.

Countries that are run on a high-skill equilibrium, such as Germany and Switzerland, tend to have highly regulated labour markets involving licence to practise and training levies (see below). They also tend to have relatively restrictive labour laws which make it difficult and expensive to fire employees. This, in turn, encourages them to make the best use that they can of the employees that they have got (Streeck, 1992). Characteristic of the high-skill economies is high productivity compared with the same sector in low-skill economies (Prais, 1995). This is true both in manufacturing and in service industries. They engage in what is sometimes called 'diversified quality production' which involves relatively short lines of high-specification products, whose specifications can be rapidly altered to meet shifts in consumer demand (Streeck, 1992), and as the example of Germany shows, they do well in the international division of labour by concentrating on segments of sectors which respond well to high-skill inputs, and are thus successful exporters despite the rise of high-volume, low-cost production in many developing countries.

## What might be done?

As has already been stated, the government has diagnosed the lack of skills as a supply problem. This is odd coming from those who are wedded to market solutions. One might wonder why signals from the market have failed to engender demand from potential employees. For some reason, it seems that there is 'market failure', so that appropriate signals fail to register. The solution is for the government to step in and ensure a steady supply of skilled workers or, at least, workers who have some vocational qualifications. But this is nonsensical, as the government's own figures demonstrate. There is limited demand for skilled workers and it is not irrational for young people to realize this and hence not to participate wholeheartedly in education, whether academic or vocational. Action needs to be taken in the first instance in relation to employers rather than young people. This does not necessarily mean that employers are 'to blame'; as we have seen, it may not make business sense for an employer to train workers. It may also not make sense to try and move 'upmarket' if there is no demand from consumers. As we saw, a 'low-skill equilibrium' is a state of affairs which is satisfactory to all parties and therefore difficult to alter.

Action by governments to incentivize employers is needed to increase the demand for skills and qualifications. Such action will have to provide either regulation for employers or rewards to them to ensure that they demand qualifications from employees. One possibility is the 'licence to practise' or demand that employees possess the appropriate qualification before they can be employed. Licence to practise already operates in some of the professions, like medicine and the law, and is common in non-professional occupations in some countries, such as Germany.[1] It was also advocated by the eighteenth-century economist Adam Smith as a way of ensuring that the workforce attained a minimum educational standard (1981, Vol. II, Bk V, pp. 786–7). The effects of a generalized licence to practise would depend on how it was framed. A modern version of Adam Smith's proposal would be to make a certain level of GCSE achievement necessary for entry into the labour market. Smith freely admitted that his proposal was not designed to enhance the skill level in the economy but to ensure that workers were not influenced by revolutionary demagogues. So one could set a certain level of academic achievement as a labour market entry threshold for civic rather than vocational purposes. This would provide a huge incentive to young people to attend to their education but would create huge opposition, not only among young people, but among employers, who would be deprived of a ready source of cheap, compliant and low-skilled labour. The labour market would become much tighter and employers would be obliged to pay employees more and find ways of utilizing effectively the skills that they had acquired. This proposal again would be sure to engender huge employer opposition.

Training levies involve a tax on employers which is put into a pool reserved for training purposes within an industrial sector. Firms have to pay and the only way in which they can recoup the levy is by using some of it to train their own employees. Employers now have an incentive to train and, since everyone is likely to, the poaching problem is diminished or eliminated. Employers are thus incentivized to make the best use of the trained employees that they have got and can do so without fear of poaching from rival firms. Levies can be either voluntary or compulsory, industry or government led. The decline of sector-imposed levies within the British economy has had an adverse effect on skill formation and it is at least arguable that the state should step in to ensure that sectors critical to the economy do raise the skill levels of their employees. A more modest proposal would be to set minimum vocational qualification levels across a range of occupations with a view to raising the skill levels in them. Employers would be obliged to engage workers with a certain level of qualification or would have to train them in order to secure a supply of labour.

One of the few certainties in British politics is that no government that is currently conceivable would dream of interfering with employer prerogatives in such ways, despite the overwhelming evidence of a skill demand problem. So this is not a solution that is likely to be implemented in the forseeable future. But refusal to act does not get rid of embarrassment given the diagnosis of the problem. Hence the problem must be framed in a different way in order to distract attention, although the latest skills White Paper (DfES, 2005b) does talk of offering a challenge to employers to take part in the design of specialized diplomas. However, the dominant discourse remains on the supply side and thus remains largely irrelevant to the upskilling agenda. The result is that the government desperately wants to be seen to be doing something about promoting a 'high-skill' and/or a 'knowledge economy' but feels itself unable to take obvious measures to do so. 'Voluntarism' remains the order of the day. Because employer participation in raising skill levels has to be without compulsion and because it has repeatedly been shown that employer enthusiasm is quite limited, the policy initiatives have, in effect, to tiptoe around the critical issue and to set up scenarios in which employers will, some-how, be persuaded of the need to raise skills. These measures include increasing the supply of information in local and regional labour markets subsidizing apprenticeship schemes, setting up sector skill councils to promote training within sectors and, most recently, encouraging employers to help design vocational diplomas in the hope that this will raise their interest in employing skilled labour.

## Vocationalism and higher education

While there is little movement in the development of skills and the take-up of vocational qualifications at level 3 and below, a striking feature of British society is the high take-up of higher education (NQF levels 4–8), some of it vocationally oriented, but much of it not. How can this be explained? We should note that an increase in academic qualifications does not equate to an increase in skills relevant to the economy (see above), so the increase in participation in higher education cannot automatically be seen as an increase in the skill level in the British economy.

A number of factors seem to be at work. First, as was pointed out in Chapter 1, there has been a long-standing divide between vocational and academic education in Britain, with vocational education traditionally lacking in prestige. Schools are influential in determining the trajectory of their pupils and there is relatively strong encouragement to go on to higher education and relatively weak encouragement to go on to vocational courses or to embark on an apprenticeship. Second, there is evidence of continuing labour market demand for graduates. This does not necessarily mean that the knowledge and skills that a university degree brings are always valuable and valued in firms, but that a degree brings positional advantage and acts as a filter in employer selection processes. One important feature of a low-skill economy is the lack of autonomy of line workers and the perceived need for management positions in the absence of self-management on the part of workers. Graduates provide a ready supply of lower and middle management personnel across a range of sectors. The government is keen not only that more young people enter higher education but that they do so through vocational routes, such as the two-year Foundation Degree (NQF level 5). However, the picture that one gets of the health of vocational qualifications is very mixed. On the one hand, certain 'weakly vocational' qualifications such as Media Studies and Sports Studies continue to be popular. On the other hand, Engineering and Chemistry, which have a clear vocational application, tend not to recruit so healthily. Subjects like Mathematics, with very strong financial returns, fail, despite this, to recruit very strongly.

Indeed, by organizing higher education as a student-driven market, the government has provided a hostage to fortune by allowing what is currently in demand or fashionable among young people to drive recruitment into universities and hence to determine the health of academic departments. Perceived national need plays a secondary role at best. This would not necessarily matter if employer demand pulled people through vocationally desirable subjects into subject departments in areas where there would be a good demand for the skills and knowledge acquired. This does not, so far, seem to have been occurring except in a limited way. It remains to be seen whether or not the significant increase in tuition fees that students will be paying from 2006 onwards will encourage students to think in a 'human capital' way and select subjects with high projected lifetime earnings premiums. One of the issues affecting student choice is the perceived difficulty of certain subjects, especially those which require relatively high levels of numeracy. There is evidence of the poor preparation of many students entering higher education in terms of numeracy and indeed literacy skills (Wilde et al., 2006). We cannot infer then, even where there is healthy recruitment to weakly vocational subjects, that there is necessarily a demand for graduates of those subjects from employers in the relevant sectors.

We likewise cannot infer, from high participation rates in higher education, that the British economy is in transition from a low- to a high-skill equilibrium. This phenomenon does tell us that there is increasing participation in the 16- to 18-year age group in full-time education, but that it is mainly driven by those moving on to higher education. The take-up of vocational level 3 qualifications continues to be weak and, as we have seen, the demand for level 3 qualifications in the labour market is projected to remain flat for some years. It would be interesting and remarkable if there were good evidence of firm demand for strongly vocational qualifications at NQF levels 4–6 (higher education up to Bachelor degree level) on the part of employers, but there is, as yet, no evidence of this. Indeed, it could only be taken as convincing evidence of an increasing demand in skills if the qualifications did indeed mark a significant increase in vocational skills and knowledge on the part of their holders. However, we know that in some sectors qualifications are offered which do not necessarily signify increased ability to do a job or to carry out that job in a significantly different way, for example Foundation Degrees for teaching assistants. The evidence that the increased uptake of level 4+ qualifications has a bearing on the skill mix in the British economy, and that it reflects an increased desire for skills on the part of British employers, is ambiguous at best.

But the shift to higher education has significant consequences for the take-up of level 3 qualifications, as we can assume that many of those who would, for example, have entered an apprenticeship are now progressing to higher education via a level 3 academic or weakly vocational qualification. A question arises therefore as to where the supply of good candidates for such qualifications is going to come from, particularly as there is evidence that suggests that there is poor progression from level 2 vocational qualifications to level 3 qualifications (DfES, 2005b). There is a danger that we could see a 'hollowing out' of the supply of suitable candidates for strongly vocational level 3 programmes even in a context of static demand.

What, finally, is the role of further education in these processes? It has to be said that it is ambiguous. The recent Foster Report on Further Education (DfES, 2005c) suggests that the role of the FE colleges should be to serve local and regional employer needs and that college missions should not be too diffuse. The traditional model of the generalist FE college that tries to do everything from entry level to level 6 work is not popular with the government. But this policy shift poses problems for this group of institutions. On the one hand, they are being asked to align themselves closely with labour market needs for vocational qualifications up to and including level 3 (and in some cases beyond); on the other hand, they are significant participants in the expansion of higher education (around 20% of student numbers), to the extent that a number of colleges now have a very significant provision of level 4+ work and are aiming towards degree awarding powers and University College status. Given participation trends and the demand problems in local and regional labour markets, this is not necessarily a poor strategy to adopt. But it is clearly one that is not very popular with the government of the day (2006).

## Conclusion

We have looked at the contrast between high- and low-skill economies and have suggested that, in comparison with other developed countries, Britain has adopted a low-skill route with weak employer demand for vocationally relevant skills and knowledge at all levels below NQF 3. This is not projected to change in the near future and we examined the main reasons why this is likely to remain the case. The increase in participation in higher education and the increase in the supply of people with qualifications at level 4 and beyond is not necessarily a counter-example to this claim. People work for qualifications for other than the strictly vocational reason of increasing workplace relevant knowledge and skills; positional advantage is significant, as is the wish to continue with some form of liberal education. The peculiarities of the British labour market suggest a continuing demand for graduates to work in lower and middle management positions without necessarily enhancing the skill base of the economy to a significant extent. Finally, these trends pose dilemmas and difficulties for the diverse further education sector which that sector will need to resolve in the next few years.

## Notes

1.  Qualifications can also lead, if not to licence to practise, at least to rights to status and pay within the workplace.

# 7 Possible Futures for VET in England

As a way of bringing together all the various strands of the previous chapters, we thought it would be useful to re-examine the key issues and problems relating to VET in England against the background of current policy directions. In this way the present and probable future state of VET might be contrasted with some suggestions for, in our view, a possible much-improved future in this sphere. In earlier chapters the key problems of VET in England were outlined in terms of the following principal themes:

- The vocational/academic divide and subordinate status of vocational programmes resulting in relatively low participation rates
- Low level of employer investment in VET and lack of a national system involving all stakeholders in planning and funding education and training
- The persistence of a low-skills equilibrium and lower levels of achievement in the vocational sphere.

Have any of these problems been solved by all the policy initiatives of the last decade or so? Well, there have been some improvements but, according to the recent White Paper on FE which reasserted the central economic mission of the sector, there are still some 'major areas of weakness' (DfES, 2006b). These are listed as follows:

> The proportion of young people staying on in education and training post-16 is scandalously low: the UK ranks 24th out of 29 developed nations. We lag well behind France and Germany in the proportion of our young adults achieving a Level 3 qualification in their early twenties. The number of

adults in the workforce without the skills at level 2 ... is much too high: in that area we rank 17th out of 30 countries. All this makes clear that as a nation we need to raise our ambitions for skills. (p. 3)

How, then, is the proposed new 'economic mission of the sector' – which is 'to equip young people and adults with the skills, competences and qualifications that employers want' (*ibid.*, p. 5) – to be achieved in terms of the reform of learning/ teaching, qualifications, organization and overall planning and funding of VET in England?

## Organising and funding VET

Writing in 1999, Green observed that:

VET in England and Wales is generally seen as one of the weakest areas of the education system, traditionally suffering from a lack of prestige and coherent planning and organi- sation. (p. 13)

In spite of what Keep (2006) has described as a 'permanent revolution' (p. 47) in VET policy initiatives in recent times, the central problems still seem to be with us. This state of affairs – in sharp contrast with the well-organized social partnership models operating in Germany and France (Skilbeck *et al.*, 1994) and, in more recent years, in the Republic of Ireland (O'Connor, 2006) – is usually explained in terms of the liberal legacy of *laissez-faire* which resulted in a voluntarist system of VET in which employers had no legal or state-prescribed role in investment or planning. Apart from two short-lived experiments in state direction – under the Industrial Training Boards from 1964 to 1973 and what has been called the 'era of MSC tripartism' (Green, 1999, p. 17) from 1973 to 1979 – the state in England has been reluctant to legislate on employers' roles in the funding and planning of VET.

What needs to be placed against this mainstream picture of traditional English voluntarism in VET is the seemingly para- doxical fact that, from primary and secondary schooling through to further and higher education and education and training in the broad learning and skills sector, the last decade or so has resulted in the English system becoming, arguably, the most centrally controlled system in the world (Bassey, 2003). Keep (2006) has recently described the present system in the following way:

> The dominant trend within the English E&T system since the early 1980s has been the increasing power of the state – in the shape of central government – to design, control and implement policy at every level across a widening range of topics ... In 1981 the role of the central state was limited and peripheral ... Today, central government and its agencies are the prime movers in the system, with other stakeholders acting in subordinate, usually minor, positions. (pp. 48–9)

A number of factors are said to have produced this centralist state of affairs, the key one being that, once the role of employers in terms of intervention, organization and funding of VET is removed from the picture, the only way the state can influence the system is by subsidizing employer training activity and establishing and expanding vocational and skills training programmes. Once this process is established, a form of internal dynamics ensures ever-increasing levels of state involvement, legislation and interventionist subsidy.

The ironic and paradoxical nature of an increasingly interventionist and centralist state in a supposedly voluntarist and *laissez-faire* system of VET can be explained in terms of deep-seated political commitments to labour market regulation (or de-regulation) and neo-liberal models of economic management. Thus, as Keep (2006) argues, 'the range of policy moves is tightly bounded by ideological no-go zones that are absent in many other developed countries' (p. 59). These ideological constraints are clearly in evidence in the FE White Paper's plans for 'meeting employer and learner needs' (DfES, 2006b, p. 7). The key policies include:

- A programme of learner accounts designed to help people gain level 3 qualifications
- An entitlement to free training for young adults aged 19–

25 without level 3 qualifications and an adult learning grant with similar aims for those over 25 on low incomes
- An extension of the Train to Gain programme which 'helps employers, supported by brokers, get training delivered in the workplace to meet their needs' (*ibid.*).

None of this signals either an end to voluntarism in VET planning and funding or the emergence of a new system of organizing and regulating the system. The key policies are reminiscent of past failures such as Training Credits and Individual Learning Accounts and – just as with the now radically diluted *Learndirect*/University for Industry strategy – the state remains as an 'animateur' or 'broker' (Hillman, 1997) through which government quangos mediate between providers and suppliers in the VET market place. Given the history of failure with such strategies the likely future in this sphere appears bleak. What about a possible future involving a completely different approach to the issues?

Here we can usefully draw on Keep's (2006) analysis of the role of the state in which he argues that:

> The English state's long-standing commitment to free-market neo-liberalism and relative deregulationist tenets renders unavailable a host of potential policy interventions used in other countries – for example, training levies, strong trade unions and statutory rights to collective bargaining on skills, strong forms of social partnership arrangement, regulated labour and product markets (such as extensive licence to practice requirements), or an industrial policy that might favour higher skill sectors. (p. 58)

Let us be more creative and imagine a possible *Education and Training Act 2010* (it would take this long for the *Speaker's Commission on Education and Training* established in 2007 to report and consult) which would include the following provisions:

1) A genuine partnership between the state (through quangos such as Local Education and Training Councils, LETCs, formerly LLSCs), employers (through sector skills councils) and trades unions which, through a

National Education and Training Council (NETC), plans, organizes, co-ordinates and funds VET of all kinds for people over the age of 14.

2) All firms will have to pay training levies based on the number of people they employ which will be used to fund work-based learning of all kinds, including apprenticeships and vocational courses in all institutions in the new Education and Training Sector (formerly the LSC).

3) The various occupational sector ETCs (formerly SSCs) – working with the appropriate vocational award bodies – will be responsible for issuing 'licences to practise' (similar to the licences for FE lecturers) without which it would be illegal to operate as a plumber, electrician, bricklayer, hairdresser, welder, etc. Licences will be issued only to people who have successfully completed approved vocational courses involving work-based elements.

All of these requirements and provisions will be enforced by the new law which governs all aspects of education and training in England. The system would, thus, be informed by examples of successful and best practice which indicate that:

> Systems based on the principle of social partnership only work when one of the partners, the state, defines the roles of the others and determines the shape of the system as a whole. (Green, 1999, p. 29)

The new ET system would, arguably, represent something far less than a sea change in the way VET is organized in England. It would, rather, consolidate and extend the best and most successful features of the present system while eliminating the least successful ones.

## VET courses and qualifications

The sometimes acrimonious debate about the best way to organize and structure educational qualifications in England was intensified in the 1990s when arguments revolved around the relative merits of a unified or stratified system (Hodgson and Spours, 1997; Hyland, 1999) Three different interest groups emerged:

*Trackers*: those who favoured something like the present system with three distinctive qualifications tracks (e.g. Prais, 1995; Raffe, 1993) based on supposed different abilities and aptitudes of students, and different goals and purposes between vocational and academic learning.

*Frameworkers*: those who support three tracks or pathways (academic/broad vocational/specific vocational) but allow for overarching frameworks such as diplomas (Dearing, 1996) to allow for flexibility and access.

*Unifiers*: those who argue for a completely unified system (Finegold *et al.*, 1990; Hodgson and Spours, 1997) which would involve a core curriculum post-16 and replace the existing qualifications structure with one single qualifications system.

There were a number of points of convergence between these three basic positions. All were agreed on the need for 14–19 reform to raise levels of achievement, trackers and unifiers both admired the general educational foundation of Continental VET schemes, and frameworks and unifiers both favoured the unitization and modularization of 14–19 education and training. At the beginning of this century the arguments for some form of unified qualifications structure became stronger, and eventually a new consensus emerged in the recommendations of the Tomlinson Committee on the reform of 14–19 curriculum and qualifications. Favouring a unifying strategy, Tomlinson (DfES, 2004a) placed emphasis on bridging the vocational/academic divide through improved and 'better vocational programmes' which would 'provide opportunities for achievement and progression in the same way as for academic studies' (p. 6). The report went on to stress that this:

Does not mean trying to fit vocational programmes into an 'academic' mould, but recognising what is distinctive and valuable about vocational learning and ensuring that it is respected and valued in its own right. (*Ibid.*)

In spite of the widespread support for these proposals, the DfES (or the New Labour government) effectively rejected the reforms with the determination to 'retain GCSEs and A levels as the cornerstones of the new system' (DfES, 2005a, p. 3). As Hodgson and Spours (2005) – both members of the Tomlinson Committee – commented in reference to the 2005 White Paper, it was yet another 'great lost opportunity' and a 'depressing example of political expediency winning out over the professional consensus for a unified and inclusive 14–19 phase' (p. 22). The FE White Paper simply restates the main principles of the 2005 statement which retains GCSEs and A-levels and, as a token to the frameworkers' aim of raising the status of vocational studies, mentioned the establishment over the coming years of 14 new overarching diplomas which will integrate aspects of GCSE and A-levels, in combination with specialized studies, functional literacy and numeracy and some work experience, and produce what are said to be qualifications suitable for either employment or further study (DfES, 2006b, p. 8). There is nothing new here and – as the recent history of qualifications reform in England demonstrates – no indication that any of this will solve the problems of VET or raise the status of vocational studies.

Given all this the *Education and Training Act 2010* would include the following provisions in relation to courses and qualifications:

1) Along with the phasing out of GNVQs which will be completed by 2008, NVQs will be phased out from all ET institutions by 2012 and returned to the workplace (their original and natural home) and function only as on-the-job workplace skill assessment strategies and not as vocational courses which will be the responsibility of approved institutions in the ET sector.

2) A licence to practise will, over a number of years, become mandatory in those sectors covered by Sector Skills Councils instituting a skilled worker grade as minimum tier with a NQF level 3 qualification (see

below). A levy system will become mandatory in order to finance part of the drive for higher basic qualifications.

3) All vocational qualifications, whether work or college based, will be required to include theory underpinning the practice and extended general education, including civic education.

## A new skills strategy?

Such legislation would underpin a radically changed skills strategy for the British economy, based on high-specification, high-quality goods and services. Britain would no longer attempt to compete on a low-paid, low-skill 'flexible' and disposable labour force, but like most of its near Continental neighbours, on a high-skill strategy. Not only would this aid the revival of British manufacturing – which, due to the rise of low-cost, low-specification manufacturers in other parts of the world, is becoming increasingly uncompetitive – but it would also lead to an improvement in the quality of services available in the UK, making it a more attractive country both for its inhabitants and for visitors.

As a consequence, vocational education would gain prestige long denied it, mainly because the public perceived, correctly, that vocational education was not in great demand by the employers in the UK. Whichever route was adopted in relation to qualifications – that of trackers, frameworkers or unifiers – vocational education would assume an importance and prestige that it has never enjoyed before in the UK.

# Bibliography

Adams, J. (1933), *Modern Developments in Educational Practice*. London: University of London Press.

—— (1996), 'Apprenticeship: A Comparative Study of the Traditional and Modern Apprenticeship'. Unpublished MA thesis. Department of Continuing Education, University of Warwick.

Ainley, P. (1988), *From School to YTS: Education and Training in England and Wales, 1944–1987*. Milton Keynes: Open University Press.

—— (1990), *Vocational Education and Training*. London: Cassell.

—— (1993), *Class and Skill*. London: Cassell.

—— (1999), *Learning Policy*. Basingstoke: Macmillan.

Ainley, P. and Bailey, B. (1997), *The Business of Learning*. London: Cassell.

Ainley, P. and Corney, M. (1990), *Training for the Future: The Rise and Fall of the Manpower Services Commission*. London: Cassell.

Ainley, P. and Rainbird, H. (eds) (1999), *Apprenticeship: Towards a New Paradigm of Learning*. London: Kogan Page.

Annett, J. and Sparrow, J. (1985), *Transfer of Learning and Training*. Sheffield: Manpower Services Commission.

Arguelles, A. and Gonczi, A. (eds) (2000), *Competency Based Education and Training: A World Perspective*. Mexico: Conalep/Noriega.

Armitage, A. *et al.* (1999), *Teaching and Training in Post-Compulsory Education*. Buckingham: Open University Press.

Ashby, E. (1958), *Technology and the Academics*. London: Macmillan.

Ashton, D. and Green, F. (1996), *Education, Training and the Global Economy*. Cheltenham: David Elgar.

Ashworth, P. D. (1992), 'Being competent and having "competencies"', *Journal of Further & Higher Education*, 16(3), 8–17.

Avis, J., Bloomer, M., Esland, G., Gleeson, D. and Hodkinson, P. (1966), *Knowledge and Nationhood: Education, Politics and Work*. London: Cassell.

Barnard, H. C. (1961), *A History of English Education from 1760*. London: University of London Press.

Barrow, R. (1987), 'Skill Talk', *Journal of Philosophy of Education*, 21(2), 187–99.

Bassey, M. (2003), 'More advocacy: give autonomy back to teachers', *BERA Newsletter*, 84, 26–30.

Bates, I. (1998), *The Competence and Outcomes Movement: The Landscape of Research*. Leeds: University of Leeds School of Education.

Bates, I. and Dutson, J. (1995), 'A Bermuda Triangle? A case study of the disappearance of competence-based vocational training policy in the context of practice', *British Journal of Education and Work*, 8(2), 41–59.

Baty, P. (1997), 'DfEE called to account', *Times Higher Education Supplement*, 14 March.

Beaumont, G. (1996), *Review of 100 NVQs and SVQs*. London: Department for Education and Employment.

Bees, M. and Swords, M. (eds) (1990), *National Vocational Qualifications and Further Education*. London: Kogan Page/National Council for Vocational Qualifications.

Bell, C. (1996), *Some Key Facts about G/NVQs Awarded*. London: Article 26.

Benjamin, H. (1975), 'The Saber-Tooth Curriculum' [1939], in Golby, M., Greenwald, J. and West, R. (eds), *Curriculum Design*. London: Croom Helm/Open University Press.

Benn, C. and Fairley, J. (eds) (1986), *Challenging the MSC on Jobs, Training and Education*. London: Pluto.

Benner, D. (2003), *Wilhelm von Humboldt's Bildungstheorie*. Weinheim and Munich: Juventa.

BIBB (Bundesinstitut für Berufsbildung) (1999), *AWEB* 'Berufliche Qualificationen – Spezialtiefbauer/bauerin'. Online www.bib.de/redaction/aweb/1999/sptief.htm (accessed February 2005).

Bloom, B. S. (1956), *Taxonomy of Educational Objectives*. London: Longman.

Bloomer, M. (1966), 'Education for Studentship', in Avis, J., Bloomer, M., Esland, G., Gleeson, D. and Hodkinson, P., *Knowledge and Nationhood: Education, Politics and Work*. London: Cassell.

Burke, J. (ed.) (1995), *Outcomes: Learning and the Curriculum*. London: Falmer.

Callender, C. (1992), *Will NVQs Work? Evidence from the Construction Industry*. Sussex: Institute of Manpower Studies, University of Sussex.

Carr, W. (1997), 'Professing Education in a Post-Modern Age', *Journal of Philosophy of Education*, 31(2), 309–27.

CBI (1989), *Towards a Skills Revolution*. London: Confederation of British Industry.

Clarke, L. and Wall, C. (1998), 'UK construction skills in the context of European developments', *Construction Management and Economics*, 16, 553–67.

Clarke, L. and Wall, C. (2000), 'Craft versus industry: the division of labour in European housing construction', *Construction Management and Economics*, 18, 689–98.

Clarke, L. and Winch, C. (eds) (2006), *Vocational Education: international approaches, developments and systems*. London: Routledge.

Coffey, D. (1992), *Schools and Work: Developments in Vocational Education*. London: Cassell.

Curtis, S. J. and Boultwood, M. E. A. (1970), *A Short History of Educational Ideas*. London: University Tutorial Press.

Dearden, R. F. (1984), *Theory and Practice in Education*. London: Routledge and Kegan Paul.

Dearden, R. F. (1990), 'Education and Training', in Esland, G. (ed.), *Education, Training and Employment*. Wokingham: Addison Wesley/ Open University Press.

Dearing, Sir R. (1996), *Review of Qualifications for 16–19 Year Olds*. Hayes: School Curriculum and Assessment Authority.

Dent, H. C. (1968), *The Education Act 1944*. London: University of London Press.

DES (1985), *The Curriculum, 5 to 16*. London: Department of Education and Science.

—— (1991), *Education and Training for the 21st Century*. London: HMSO.

Dewey, J. (1966), *Democracy and Education* [1916]. New York: Free Press.

DfEE (1997), *First Steps in Upgrading NVQs*. London: Department for Education and Employment.

—— (1998), *The Learning Age: A Renaissance for a New Britain*. London: Department for Education and Employment.

—— (2000a), *Colleges for Excellence and Innovation*. London: Department for Education and Employment.

—— (2000b), *Skills for All: Research Report from the National Skills Task Force*. London: Department for Education and Employment.

—— (2001), *Opportunity and Skills in the Knowledge-Driven Economy*. London: Department for Education and Employment.

DfES (2001), *New Plans for Modern Apprenticeships*. London: Department for Education and Skills.

—— (2002a), *Vocational Qualifications 2000/2001*. London: Department for Education and Skills.

—— (2002b), *Participation in Education, Training and Employment by 16–18 Year Olds in England: 2000 and 2001*. London: Department for Education and Skills. Online www.dfes.gov.uk/rsgateway/DB/SFR/ (accessed June 2004).

—— (2003), *The Economic Benefits of Education*. London: Department for Education and Skills.

DfES (2004a), *14–19 Curriculum and Qualifications Reform*. London: Department for Education and Skills.

—— (2004b), *Participation in Education, Training and Employment by 16–18 Year Olds in England: 2002 and 2003*. London: Department for Education and Skills. Online www.dfes.gov.uk/rsgateway/DB/SFR/ (accessed June 2004).

—— (2005a), *14–19 Education and Skills*. London: Department for Education and Skills.

—— (2005b), *14–19 Skills Summary*. London: Department for Education and Skills.

—— (2005c), *Realising the Potential: A Review of the Future Role of Further Education Colleges*. Nottingham: Department for Education and Skills Publications.

—— (2006a), *Vocational Qualifications in the UK 2004/2005*. London: Department for Education and Skills.

—— (2006b), *Further Education: Raising Skills, Improving Life Chances*. Nottingham: Department for Education and Skills Publications.

DOE (1981), *A New Training Initiative – A Programme for Action*. London: HMSO.

DOE/DES (1986), *Working Together – Education and Training*. London: HMSO.

Dore, R. (1976), *The Diploma Disease*. London: Allen & Unwin.

Ecclestone, K. (2004), 'Learning or Therapy? The Demoralisation of Education', *British Journal of Educational Studies*, 52(2), 112–37.

ED (1993), *Systems and Procedures of Certification of Qualifications in the United Kingdom*. Sheffield: Employment Department Methods Strategy Group.

Elliott, J. (1993), *Reconstructing Teacher Education*. London: Falmer.

Ernst and Young (1995), *The Evaluation of Modern Apprenticeship Prototypes*. Sheffield: Centre for the Study of Post–16 Developments, University of Sheffield.

Esland, G. (ed.) (1990), *Education, Training and Employment*. Wokingham: Addison Wesley/Open University Press.

Evans, B. (1992), *The Politics of the Training Market*. London: Routledge.

Farley, M. (1983), 'Trends and Structural Changes in English Vocational Education', in Watson, K. (ed.), *Youth, Education and Employment: International Perspectives*. London: Croom Helm.

Farlie, V. (2004), 'Are apprenticeships any longer a credible vocational route for young people, and can the supply side respond effectively to government policy, and address the needs of learners and employers'. Online www.nuffield14-19review.org.uk/cgi/documents/documents. cgi?a=52&t=template.htm (accessed April 2006).

FEFC (1994), *NVQs in the Further Education Sector in England*. Coventry: Further Education Funding Council.

FEU (1982), *Basic Skills*. London: Further Education Unit.

Field, J. (1995), 'Reality Testing in the Workplace: Are NVQs Employment Led?', in Hodkinson, P. and Issitt, M. (eds) (1995), *The Challenge of Competence*. London: Cassell.

Finegold, D. (1991), 'Institutional Incentives and Skill Creation: Preconditions for a High-Skill Equilibrium', in Ryan, P. (ed.), *International Comparisons of Vocational Education and Training for Intermediate Skills*. Hove: Falmer Press, pp. 93–116.

—— (1999), 'Education, training and economic performance in comparative perspective', in Flude, M. and Sieminski, S. (eds), *Education, Training and the Future of Work: Vol. II*. London: Routledge/Open University Press.

Finegold, D. *et al.* (1990), *A British Baccalaureate: Overcoming Divisions between Education and Training*. London: Institute for Public Policy Research.

Finegold, D. and Soskice, D. (1988), 'The Failure of Training in Britain: Analysis and Prescription', *Oxford Review of Economic Policy*, 4(1), 21–53.

Finn, D. (1986), 'YTS, the Jewel in the MSC's Crown?', in Benn, C. and Fairley, J. (eds), *Challenging the MSC on Jobs, Training and Education*. London: Pluto.

Fletcher, S. (1991), *NVQs, Standards and Competence*. London: Kogan Page.

Flude, M. and Sieminski, S. (eds) (1999), *Education, Training and the Future of Work: Vol. II*. London: Routledge/Open University Press.

Foreman-Peck, J. (2004), 'Spontaneous Disorder? A Very Short History of British Vocational Education and Training, 1563–1973', *Policy Futures in Education*, 2(1), 72–101.

Géhin, J.-P. (2006), 'Vocational Education (VET) in France: A Turbulent History and Peripheral Role', in Clarke, L. and Winch, C. (eds), *Vocational Education*. London: Routledge.

Goddard, P. (ed.) (1999), *Paul Dirac: The Man and His Work*. Cambridge: Cambridge University Press.

Gospel, H. (1995), 'The Decline of Apprenticeship Training in Britain', *Industrial Relations Journal*, 26(1), 32–44.

—— (1998a), 'The Revival of Apprenticeship Training in Britain', *British Journal of Industrial Relations*, 36(3), 435–57.

—— (1998b), 'Reinventing Apprenticeship', *Centrepiece*, 3(3), 19–23.

Gospel, H. and Fuller, A. (1998), 'The Modern Apprenticeship: new wine in old bottles?' *Human Resource Management Journal*, 8(1), 5–22.

Lea, J., Hayes, D., Armitage, A., Lomas, L. and Markless, S. (2003), *Working in Post-Compulsory Education*. Maidenhead: Open University Press.

Leach, A. F. (1904), *The Schools of Medieval England*. London: The Antiquary's Books.

Leathwood, C. (1998), 'Irrational Bodies and Corporate Culture: further education in the 1990s', *International Journal of Inclusive Education*, 2(3), 255–68.

Lee, D., Marsden, D., Rickman, P. and Duncombe, J. (1990), *Scheming for Youth: A Study of YTS in the Enterprise Culture*. Milton Keynes: Open University Press.

Lee, H. D. P. (trans.) (1965), *Plato – The Republic*. Harmondsworth: Penguin.

Lees, D. and Chiplin, R. (1970), 'The economics of industrial training', *Lloyds Bank Review*, April, 35–41.

Lester Smith, W. O. (1966), *Education: An Introductory Survey*. Harmondsworth: Penguin.

Lewis, T. (1991), 'Difficulties attending the New Vocationalism in the USA', *Journal of Philosophy of Education*, 25(1), 95–108.

Lewis, T. (2006), 'School Reform in America: Can Dewey's Ideas Save High School Vocational Education?', in Clarke, L. and Winch, C. (eds), *Vocational Education*. London: Routledge.

LSC (2001a), *LSC to Lead on Modern Apprenticeships*. London: Learning and Skills Council.

LSC (2001b), *Learning and Skills Council: Strategic Framework to 2004 – Corporate Plan*. Coventry: Learning and Skills Council.

LSC (2005a), *Further Education, Work-based Learning for Young People and Adult and Community Learning – Learner Numbers in England 2004/5*. London: Learning and Skills Council.

LSC (2005b), *Transforming Learning and Skills: Our Annual Statement of Priorities*. Coventry: Learning and Skills Council.

Maclure, S. (1973), *Educational Documents*. London: Methuen.

—— (1991), *Missing Links: The Challenge to Further Education*. London: Policy Studies Institute.

Marks, J. (1996), *Vocational Education, Qualifications and Training in Britain*. London: Institute of Economic Affairs.

Marx, K. (1970), *Capital* [1887]. London: Lawrence & Wishart.

Matlay, H. and Hyland, T. (1997), 'NVQs in the small business sector: a critical overview', *Education and Training*, 39(9), 325–32.

McCulloch, G. (1986), 'Policy, Politics and Education – TVEI', *Journal of Education Policy*, 1(1), 35–52.

Mitchell, L. (1989), 'The Definition of Standards and their Assessment',

Green, A. (1990), *Education and State Formation*. London: Macmillan.

—— (1995), 'The European Challenge to British Vocational Education and Training', in Hodkinson, P. and Issitt, M. (eds), *The Challenge of Competence*. London: Cassell.

—— (1996), 'Education and the Development State in Asia', in Centre For Labour Market Studies, MSc in Training, *Module 3*, Units 1, 2, pp. 251–70.

—— (1997), 'Core Skills, General Education and Unification in Post-16 Education', in Hodgson, A. and Spours, K. (eds), *Dearing and Beyond: 14–19 Qualifications, Frameworks and Systems*. London: Kogan Page.

—— (1999), 'The roles of the state and the social partners in vocational education and training systems', in Flude, M. and Sieminski, S. (eds), *Education, Training and the Future of Work: Vol. II*. London: Routledge/Open University Press.

Green, A. and Lucas, N. (eds) (1999), *FE and Lifelong Learning: Realigning the Sector for the Twenty-First Century*. London: University of London Institute of Education.

Green, A., Wolf, A. and Leney, T. (1999), *Convergence and Divergence in European Education and Training Systems*. London: Institute of Education.

Greinert, W.-D. (2006), 'The German Philosophy of Vocational Education', in Clarke, L. and Winch, C. (eds), *Vocational Education*. London: Routledge.

Gribble, J. (1969), *Introduction to Philosophy of Education*. Boston, MA: Allyn and Bacon.

Griffiths, M. (1987), 'The teaching of skills and the skills of teaching', *Journal of Philosophy of Education*, 21(2), 203–14.

Grugulis, I. (2002), *Skill and Qualifications: The Contribution of NVQs to Raising Skill Levels*. Warwick: SKOPE Research Project No. 36, University of Warwick.

Hall, V. (1994), *Further Education in the UK*. Bristol: Collins Educational/ Staff College.

Halsey, A., Heath, A. and Ridge, J. (1980), *Origins and Destinations: Family, Class and Education in Modern Britain*. Oxford: Oxford University Press.

Hanf, G. (2006), 'Under American Influence? The Making of Modern German Training in Large Berlin Enterprises at the Beginning of the 20th Century', in Clarke, L. and Winch, C. (eds), *Vocational Education*. London: Routledge.

Hart, J. (1998), 'Report urges training overhaul', *Times Educational Supplement*, 30 October.

Hart, W. A. (1978), 'Against Skills', *Oxford Review of Education*, 4(2), 205–16.

Hayes, D. (2003), 'The Changed Nexus Between Work and Education', in Lea, J. Hayes, D., Armitage, A., Lomas, L. and Markless, S., *Working in Post-Compulsory Education*. Maidenhead: Open University Press.

Hayward, G. (2004), 'The Decline of Vocational Learning in England', *bwp@*, 7. Online www.bwpat.de/7eu/hayward_uk_bwpat7.shtml (accessed April 2006).

HEFCE (2004), *FE/HE Practitioner Group Report on Mixed Economy Provision*. London: Higher Education Funding Council for England.

Hillier, Y. and Jameson, J. (2003), *Researching Post-Compulsory Education*. London: Continuum.

Hillman, J. (1997), *University for Industry: Creating a National Learning Network*. London: Institute for Public Policy Research.

HM Treasury (2000), *Productivity in the UK: The Evidence and the Government's Approach*. Online www.hm-treasury.gov.uk/media/D4A/E5/ACF1FBA.pdf (accessed May 2006).

Hoare, S. (2006), 'That'll Do Nicely', *Education Guardian*, 7 March, 27.

Hodgson, A. and Spours, K. (eds) (1997), *Dearing and Beyond: 14–19 Qualifications, Frameworks and Systems*. London: Kogan Page.

Hodgson, A. and Spours, K. (2005), 'Anger, analysis and creative thinking', *Adults Learning*, 16(8), 22–3.

Hodkinson, P. (1997), 'A Lethal Cocktail: NVQs, small employers and payment by results', *Educa*, 169, January, 7–8.

Hodkinson, P. and Issitt, M. (eds) (1995), *The Challenge of Competence*. London: Cassell.

Holland, R. F. (1980), *Against Empiricism: On Education, Epistemology and Value*. Oxford: Basil Blackwell.

Holt, M. (ed.) (1987), *Skills and Vocationalism: The Easy Answer*. Milton Keynes: Open University Press.

Hyland, T. (1993) 'Competence, Knowledge and Education', *Journal of Philosophy of Education*, 27(1), 57–68.

—— (1994), *Competence, Education and NVQs: Dissenting Perspectives*. London: Cassell.

—— (1998), 'Exporting Failure: the strange case of NVQs and overseas markets', *Educational Studies*, 34(3), 369–80.

—— (1999), *Vocational Studies, Lifelong Learning and Social Values*. Aldershot: Ashgate.

—— (2003), 'Work-Based Learning Programmes and Social Capital', *Journal of In-Service Education*, 29(1), 49–60.

—— (2005), 'Learning and Therapy: Oppositional or Complementary Processes?', *Adults Learning*, 16(5), 16–17.

—— (2006a), 'Vocational Education and Training and the Therapeutic Turn', *Educational Studies*, 32(2), 299–306.

Hyland, T. (2006b), 'Swimming Against the Tide: Behaviou Reductionism in the Harmonisation of European Higher Educat Systems', *Prospero*, 12(1), 24–30.

Hyland, T. and Johnson, S. (1998), 'Of Cabbages and Key Ski exploding the mythology of core transferable skills in post-scho education', *Journal of Further & Higher Education*, 22(2), 163–72.

Hyland, T. and Merrill, B. (2003), *The Changing Face of Further Educatio* London: RoutledgeFalmer.

Hyland, T. and Weller, P. (1994), *Implementing NVQs in FE Colleges* Warwick: Continuing Education Research Centre, University o Warwick.

IES (1995), *Employers' Use of the NVQ System*. Sussex: Institute of Employment Studies, University of Sussex.

Iversen, T. (2005), *Capitalism, Welfare and Democracy*. Cambridge: Cambridge University Press.

Jessup, G. (1990), 'National Vocational Qualifications: Implications for Further Education', in Bees, M. and Swords, M. (eds), *National Vocational Qualifications and Further Education*. London: Kogan Page/ National Council for Vocational Qualifications.

—— (1991), 'Implications for Individuals: the Autonomous Learner', in Jessup, G. (ed.), *Outcomes: NVQs and the Emerging Model of Education and Training*. Brighton: Falmer.

Jessup, G. (ed.) (1991), *Outcomes: NVQs and the Emerging Model of Education and Training*. London: Falmer.

Johnson, S. (1998), 'Skills, Socrates and the Sophists: Learning from History', *British Journal of Educational Studies*, 46(2), 201–13.

Jonathan, R. (1987), 'The Youth Training Scheme and Core Skills: an educational analysis', in Holt, M. (ed.), *Skills and Vocationalism: The Easy Answer*. Milton Keynes: Open University Press.

Keep, E. (2006), 'State Control of the English Education and Training System – playing with the biggest train set in the world', *Journal of Vocational Education and Training*, 58(1), 47–64.

Kenneth Richmond, W. (1945), *Education in England*. Harmondsworth: Penguin.

Kerschensteiner, G. (1964/1968), *Staatsbürgerliche Erziehung für der deutschen Jugend* [1901], in *Ausgewählte Pädagogische Texte*, Band 1. Paderborn: Ferdinand Schöningh.

Kerschensteiner, G. (1968), *Silten, Gebränche, Kulte als Wertträger im Bildungsverfahren* [1925], in *Ausgewählte Pädagogische Texte*, Band 2. Paderborn: Ferdinand Schöningh.

Lawson, J. and Silver, H. (1978), *A Social History of Education in England*. London: Methuen.

in Burke, J. (ed.), *Competency Based Education and Training*. London: RoutledgeFalmer.

MSC (1977), *Training for Skills*. Sheffield: Manpower Services Commission.

Musgrave, P. W. (1964), 'The Definition of Technical Education, 1860–1910', *The Vocational Aspect of Secondary and Further Education*, 34(1), 105–11.

Musgrave, P. W. (ed.) (1970), *Sociology, History and Education*. London: Methuen.

NCC (1990), *Core Skills 16–19*. York: National Curriculum Council.

NCVQ (1989), *Initial Criteria and Guidelines for Staff Development*. London: National Council for Vocational Qualifications.

NCVQ (1991), *Criteria for National Vocational Qualifications*. London: National Council for Vocational Qualifications.

NCVQ (1992), *Response to Consultation on GNVQs*. London: National Council for Vocational Qualifications.

Nelson-Jones, R. (1989), *Human Relationship Skills*. London: Cassell.

Nichols, A. (1998), 'Too much fuss and bother?', *Times Educational Supplement*, 19 June.

Nuffield Foundation (2005), *The Nuffield Review of 14–19 Education and Training, 1st Annual Report*. London: Nuffield Foundation.

Oates, T. (2004), 'The Role of Outcomes-Based National Qualifications in the Development of an Effective Vocational Education and Training System: the case of England and Wales', *Policy Futures in Education*, 2(1), 53–71.

O'Connor, L. (2006), 'Meeting the skills needs of a buoyant economy: apprenticeship – the Irish experience', *Journal of Vocational Education and Training*, 58(1), 31–46.

Ong, W. J. (1970), 'Latin Language Study as a Renaissance Puberty Rite', in Musgrave, P. W. (ed.), *Sociology, History and Education*. London: Methuen.

Parkin, N. (1978), 'Apprenticeships: Outmoded or Undervalued?', *Personnel Management*, 10(5), 22–46.

Pen, J. (1970), *Modern Economics*. London: Pelican.

Peters, R. S. (1978), 'Ambiguities in Liberal Education and the Problem of its Content', in Strike, K. A. and Egan, K. (eds), *Ethics and Educational Policy*. London: Routledge and Kegan Paul.

Pinker, S. (1998), *How the Mind Works*. Harmondsworth: Penguin.

Plumb, J. H. (1961), *England in the Eighteenth Century*. Harmondsworth: Penguin.

Prais, S. (1995), *Productivity, Education and Training: An International Perspective*. Cambridge: Cambridge University Press.

Prais, S. J., Jarvis, V. and Wagner, K. (1989), 'Productivity and Vocational Skills in Services in Britain and Germany: Hotels', *National Institute Economic Review*, November, 52–74.

Pring, P. (1995), *Closing the Gap: Liberal Education and Vocational Preparation*. London: Hodder & Stoughton.

QAA (2001), *The Framework for Higher Education Qualifications in England, Wales and Northern Ireland*. London: Quality Assurance Agency.

QCA (2004a), *Evaluation of Technical Certificates in Modern Apprenticeships*. London: Qualifications and Curriculum Authority.

QCA (2004b), *The Structure of the NQF*. London: Qualifications and Curriculum Authority.

Raffe, D. (1993), 'Tracks and Pathways: Differentiation in Education and Training Systems and their Relation to the Labour Market'. Paper presented to the First European Conference of the European Research Network on Transitions in Youth. Barcelona, Spain.

Raggatt, P. (1994), 'Implementing NVQs in colleges: progress, perceptions and issues', *Journal of Further & Higher Education*, 16(1), 59–74.

Raggatt, P. and Williams, S. (1999), *Government, Markets and Vocational Qualifications*. London: Falmer.

Rikowski, G. (1998), *Three Types of Apprenticeship: Three Forms of Mastery*. Birmingham: School of Education, Birmingham University.

Roe, P., Wiseman, J. and Costello M. (2006), *Perceptions and Use of NVQs: A Survey of Employers in England*. Nottingham: Department for Education and Skills Publications.

Ryan, P. (2004), 'Apprentice Strikes in the Twentieth-Century UK Engineering and Shipbuilding Industries', *Historical Studies in Industrial Relations*, 18, 1–6.

Salvemini, G. (1965), *The French Revolution 1788–1792*. London: Jonathan Cape.

Sanderson, M. (1994), *The Missing Stratum: Technical Education in England, 1900–1990*. London: Athlone Press.

Schofield, H. (1972), *The Philosophy of Education – An Introduction*. London: Allen & Unwin.

Schofield, P. (1923), 'Training and the Young Worker', *Welfare Work*, 4(426), 15–21.

Senker, P. (1992), *Industrial Training in a Cold Climate*. Aldershot: Avebury.

Sheldrake, J. and Vickerstaff, S. (1987), *The History of Industrial Training in Britain*. Godstone, Surrey: Avebury.

Sherlock, D. (1999), 'Modern Apprenticeship and national traineeship – raising standards', speech at the Training for Young People, Skills for the Millennium Conference. Leicester: TEC National Council.

Silver, H. and Brennan, J. (1988), *A Liberal Vocationalism*. London: Methuen.

Simon, B. (1974), *Education and the Labour Movement, 1870–1920*. London: Lawrence & Wishart.

Sinclair, T. A. (trans.) (1962), *Aristotle – The Politics*. Harmondsworth: Penguin.

Skilbeck, M., Connell, H., Lowe, N. and Tait, K. (1994), *The Vocational Quest: New Directions in Education and Training*. London: Routledge.

Skills and Enterprise Network (1997), *Modern Apprenticeships – A Success Story*. London: Department for Education and Employment.

Smith, A. (1981), *An Inquiry into the Nature and Causes of the Wealth of Nations*, Vols I and II, ed. R. H. Campbell and A. S. Skinner. Indianapolis, IN: Liberty Fund.

Smith, M. (1984), 'Mental Skills: some critical reflections', *Journal of Philosophy of Education*, 16(3), 225–32.

Smith, R. (1987), 'Skills – the middle way', *Journal of Philosophy of Education*, 21(2), 197–201.

Smithers, A. (1993), *All our Futures: Britain's Education Revolution*. London: Channel 4 Televison 'Dispatches' Report on Education.

Smithers, A. (1996), *Comments on the Beaumont Report*. London: Institute of Commercial Management.

Stanton, G. (2004), 'The organisation of full-time 14–19 provision in the state sector'. Online www.nuffield14–19review.org.uk/cgi/documents/documents.cgi?a=30&t=template.htm (accessed April 2006).

Stewart, J. and Sambrook, S. (1995), 'The role of functional analysis in NVQs: a critical appraisal', *British Journal of Education and Work*, 8(2), 93–106.

Streeck, W. (1992), *Social Institutions and Economic Performance*. London: Sage.

TA (1990), *Enterprise in Higher Education*. Sheffield: Training Agency.

TSO (2003), *21st Century Skills: Realising Our Potential – Individuals, Employers, Nation*, Cm 5810. London: The Stationery Office.

Tuxworth, E. (1989), 'Competence-based Education and Training: background and origins', in Burke, J. (ed.), *Competency Based Education and Training*. London: RoutledgeFalmer.

UDACE (1989), *Understanding Competence*. Leicester: Unit for the Development of Adult Continuing Education.

University of Sussex (1996), *The Assessment of NVQs*. Sussex: Institute of Education, University of Sussex.

Unwin, L. and Wellington, J. (2001), *Young People's Perspectives on Education, Training and Employment*. London: Kogan Page.

Waks, L. (2004), 'Workplace Learning in America: Shifting roles of households, schools and firms', *Educational Philosophy and Theory*, 36, 5.

Walsh, P. D. (1978), 'Upgrading Practical Subjects', *Journal of Further & Higher Education*, 2(3), 58–71.

Warhurst, C., Grugulis, I. and Keep, E. (eds) (2004), *The Skills That Matter*. London: Palgrave.

Westerhuis, A. (2006), 'The Role of the State in Vocational Education: A Political Analysis of the History of Vocational Education in the Netherlands', in Clarke, L. and Winch, C. (eds), Vocational Education. London: Routledge.

White, J. (1997), *Education and the End of Work*. London: Cassell.

Wilde, S., Wright, S., Hayward, G., Johnson, J. and Skerrett, R. (2006), *Nuffield Review Higher Education Focus Groups Preliminary Report*. Online www.nuffield14-19review.org.uk/files/documents106–1.pdf (accessed May 2006).

Wilds, E. H. and Lottich, K. V. (1970), *The Foundations of Modern Education*. New York: Holt, Rinehart and Winston.

Wilkinson, E. (1931), 'Co-operation between Education and Industry', *Labour Management*, 8(133), 240–8.

Williams, G. (1963), *Apprenticeship in Europe: The Lesson for Britain*. London: Chapman & Hall.

Williams, K. (1994), 'Vocationalism and Liberal Education: exploring the tensions', *Journal of Philosophy of Education*, 28(1), 89–100.

Williams, M. (2000), *Wealth without Nations*. London: Athol Books.

Williams, R. (1961), *The Long Revolution*. Harmondsworth: Penguin.

Wilson, J. (1972), *Philosophy and Educational Research*. Slough: National Foundation for Educational Research.

Winch, C. (1995), 'Education Needs Training', *Oxford Review of Education*, 21(3), 315–25.

—— (2000), *Education, Work and Social Capital*. London: Macmillan.

—— (2006), 'Georg Kerschensteiner – founding the dual system in Germany', *Oxford Review of Education*, 32(3), 381–96.

Wolf, A. (1995), *Competence-Based Assessment*. Buckingham: Open University Press.

# Index